ONE BOOK - ALL BUZZWORDS

Authors
Etienne Kneschke & Simon Geisenberger

AF209040

Mission Possible: The Process Excellence Enterprise

'HOUSTON, WE HAVE PROBLEM!'

THE BOOK IS A SPRINT! THE EXECUTION IS A MARATHON!

A Guidebook for Process
Intelligence & Excellence

This book is the result of years of BPM experience. Many thanks to all process management and excellence enthusiasts from various sectors and industries who have maintained an intensive exchange with us over many years and to all friends and colleagues who support and challenge us in establishing excellent process management.

ONE BOOK - ALL BUZZWORDS

,

METHODS & TOOLS
LEAN SIX SIGMA
CHANGE MANAGEMENT
ROBOTIC PROCESS AUTOMATION
INTEGRATED MANAGEMENT SYSTEM
BUSINESS PROCESS IMPROVEMENT PROCESS
TRANSFORMATION **BPM BOARD & COMMITTEE**
COMPLEXITY PROCESS MODEL & ARCHITECTURE **TOP-DOWN**
PROCESS PERFORMANCE INDICATOR **BUSINESS INTELLIGENCE**
CORPORATE STRATEGY CENTER OF PROCESS EXCELLENCE
PROCESS MINING FLOW CHART **VISION, MISSION, CORPORATE VALUES**
ARTIFICIAL INTELLIGENCE PROCESS OWNER ENTERPRISE CAPABILITIES
TECHNOLOGY **CHIEF PROCESS OFFICER** TARGET OPERATING MODEL
PROCESS EXCELLENCE ENTERPRISE
BUSINESS PROCESS MANAGEMENT SOFTWARE ROLES & RESPONSIBILITIES
ORGANISATIONAL STRUCTURE **GOVERNANCE** SPONSORSHIP
KEY PERFORMANCE INDICATOR BPMN2.0 PROCESS INTELLIGENCE REPORTING
BUSINESS PROCESS MANAGEMENT INTERNET OF THINGS
ENTERPRISE CAPABILITY MATURITY MODEL **BUSINESS PROCESS MANAGER**
WORKFLOW DIAGRAM **PROCESS EXCELLENCE COMMUNITY**
WORKFLOW MANAGEMENT SYSTEM **BOTTOM-UP** CULTURE
DIGITAL TRANSFORMATION ENABLEMENT & TRAINING
PROCESS REENGINEERING **END-TO-END PROCESS**
EFFICIENCY & EFFECTIVENESS
DATA QUALITY & INTEGRATION
CORPORATE GOALS
VALUE CHAIN

A Guidebook for Process
Intelligence & Excellence

Bibliographic information published by the Deutsche Nationalbibliothek
The Deutsche Nationalbibliothek lists this publication in the Deutsche Nationalbibliografie; detailed bibliographic data are available in the Internet at https://dnb.dnb.de

Publisher: BoD • Books on Demand GmbH, In de Tarpen 42, 22848 Norderstedt
Print: Libri Plureos GmbH, Friedensallee 273, 22763 Hamburg

DE ISBN: 978-3-7597-0766-6 (print)
DE ISBN: 978-3-7597-3968-1 (ebook)
EN ISBN: 978-3-7597-8663-0 (print)

Everything follows a process, including this book.

Table of contents

A. Preface

Hammer and Champy described crises, change, digitalisation and the fast pace of our business world in their book 'REEN-GINEERING THE COOPERATION' in the Early 1990s, calling for a radical change in processes. More than 30 years have passed since then, and a closer look at many organisations shows that neither a transformation nor a process reengineering has occurred. On the contrary, processes have taken on a life of their own and become even more complicated. Software providers and consulting companies have taken advantage of this for decades, have grown enormously and have enriched themselves. In addition, growth and globalisation have become more critical in recent years and have compensated for inadequacies and waste.

One of the reasons for this is that fundamental changes and transformations in human evolution have always taken place over long periods, and the acceptance and understanding of these fundamental changes take time. But what happens when growth and globalisation can no longer bear the resulting costs and, at the same time, supply chains and regulations become ever more demanding? In addition, artificial intelligence and many other innovative technologies are creating new opportunities that will have an even more significant impact on the transformation and collaboration between humans and technology. Unfortunately, this will make it even more difficult for some organisations to drive change, as they have missed at least one stage of organisational and process evolution in recent decades and now need to make more giant leaps.

But what exactly is the next step? Ultimately, it is about connecting and expanding competencies and skills, especially those that do not relate to the traditional areas of direct value creation. It's about overcoming departmental boundaries and silos that stand in the way of genuine and honest collaboration. The more humans share and interconnect their experience and knowledge, the more they work towards common goals and allow different perspectives, and the more innovative, customer-oriented and efficient organisations will become.

In reality, however, such cross-functional collaboration rarely occurs, and where it is claimed, it is more lip service than real collaboration. As a result, many organisations believe they collaborate internally across all areas and are surprised that their desired improvements have yet to be achieved. This collaboration is an illusion that requires a change in culture and organisational structures. One of the hopes of process excellence is to improve this very collaboration. However, process excellence is not a magic pill, and of course, the introduction of process excellence is not an easy journey without ups and downs, bumps, and pains. Consistent and tough decisions need to be made that benefit everyone. Responsibilities, competencies and processes must be adapted and, in most cases, transformed. Furthermore, resistance must be endured until a change in thinking sets in.

Change strategies as we know them will only be partially justified because we need much more to tackle the complex problems of our time. Ultimately, it is about transformation, not just change and optimisation.

Crises and other challenges are still being dealt with using traditional change strategies such as repair and patching. This is how traditional change management takes place, but not transformation, because **transformation follows a different logic from conventional change.** Therefore, reorganising processes and business models will require new strategies and approaches across all sectors.

Transformation is like the journey of a caterpillar turning into a butterfly. It is a profound process of fundamental change and growth. It is a complete metamorphosis where the old form is shed, and a new form emerges. Just as a caterpillar transforms into a butterfly, transformation in life is often about shedding old habits, beliefs or limitations and embracing new perspectives, opportunities and personal growth. If nature used traditional change strategies for this process, it would attempt to attach wings to the caterpillar, and we would never witness the emergence of beautiful, colourful butterflies. Neither the caterpillar nor the butterfly is better or worse because both are necessary and part of the transformative process. So you always have to realise where you come from, where you are and what has ultimately made or will make you a butterfly.

The transformation process usually starts very slowly. We encounter anomalies daily and realise that things can't go on like this, so we question things. The path of transformation is not mapped out and is associated with uncertainties. Radical change, therefore, requires strong determination, diverse perspectives and ideas, and an open culture of discussion and debate. Even though the transformation process is a long journey that cannot be fully predicted, it involves several crucial factors that make such a journey much more efficient and cost-effective and avoid detours.

This book only claims to detail some aspects of this paradigm shift. It provides an overview of the interrelationships, ideas, initial approaches, and suggestions so everyone can begin their transformation process.

'As machines become better machines, enterprises need to start becoming better enterprises!'

Etienne and Simon

B. Introduction

Let's ⊃ start with an analogy. In the infinite vastness of the cosmos, where the stars sparkle like scattered diamonds, there was a spaceship like no other, the 'Enterprise'. It was a marvel of technology and human ingenuity. For years, it had travelled through the galaxies, venturing into the unknown and searching for answers to the mysteries beyond our reach. With a crew of brilliant minds and fearless explorers, the spaceship Enterprise embarked on countless missions, each more daring than the last. The Enterprise was a beacon of hope and a testament to the limitless potential of humanity.

The reputation of the spaceship Enterprise grew with every successful expedition, and its crew became legendary. They were pioneers who pushed the boundaries of what was possible and made discovery after discovery in the universe. Their names were whispered in awe and reverence, and their stories were immortalised in the annals of space exploration. The spaceship's success inspired generations and ignited a passion for exploration and discovery that would shape the future of humanity. The Enterprise had explored and conquered the universe, igniting curiosity and wonder.

Over time, other civilisations and spacefaring peoples were inspired by the spaceship's remarkable achievements, and soon, attempts were made to replicate their successes. Countless experts and researchers from various planets and star systems dedicated their lives to exploring and understanding the intricacies of the spaceship. They tried to unlock its secrets, hoping to replicate its capabilities in their ships. But despite their efforts, they could not match the ingenuity and technical skills of the original.

Nevertheless, these experiments were not in vain. They may not have reached the original level of innovation, but they brought significant progress in their own way. Many new spaceships were created, each incorporating elements of the original ship. These spaceships were characterised by higher speed, improved manoeuvrability and increased efficiency and effectiveness.

The space industry saw a growing number of emerging competitors, making it increasingly difficult for established players to retain their competitive edge. These new entrants brought new perspectives, innovative approaches and often significant financial support, posing a threat to the traditional giants of the space industry. In addition, difficulties arose in dealing with new technologies and regulations. Progress in space technology was happening at an incredible pace. There were breakthroughs in propulsion systems, materials science and automation. While these advancements have opened up exciting opportunities, integrating them into existing technologies has been a major challenge.

While improving the original spaceship, the crew of engineers and scientists encountered various challenges. Everyone focused on their respective areas and worked tirelessly to improve the ship's performance. However, as more and more deviations and errors emerged, the task of integrating all the improvements became increasingly complex. Investment increased by leaps and bounds, and the crew realised that tackling these *issues required significant resources. The improvements that had been expected to progress quickly began to slow down and stutter in their implementation. The crew needed help to keep up with the increasing technical difficulties and the ever-growing opportunities.*

*With each new technology and capability that was introduced, the crew faced enormous new problems. A change in one area often let to unforeseen consequences in another. The space-ship became a complex puzzle whose pieces were constantly shifting and evolving. It became increasingly difficult to accurately predict the effects of each change. That was the moment when it echoed through the halls: '**Houston, we have a problem!**' It's a challenging and complex situation for everyone, but with so much experience and ambitious crew members, there has to be a solution! .... So let's get on with it.*

Thousands of organisations are struggling with the challenges of the spaceship Enterprise. They are looking for a recipe that describes how the individual new and old ingredients can be ideally combined and processed because the (digital) transformation will significantly change the way organisations work and function.

As new technologies reshape industries and business models, organisations must overcome complex challenges and find innovative solutions in a disruptive world. Traditional siloed and function-oriented organisations are replaced by more agile, dynamic, and process-oriented structures focusing on cross-functional collaboration and integration. To succeed and keep pace in the digital age, profound changes to an organisation's skills and capabilities and the introduction of new technologies are required.

By recognising the potential of 'digital' transformation, they can increase operational efficiency, improve the customer experience and gain a competitive advantage. Successful organisations, therefore, deal proactively with complexity and use it as an opportunity to drive growth and revolutionise their digital development. However, this can only be done with restructuring and reorganisation and can (or will) lead to resistance to change, which an organisation must withstand!

This paradigm shift, therefore, requires careful change management strategies that effectively address the human and technical aspects of organisational change. Organisations must also find the right balance between people, structure, process, and technology to do justice to the complexity of their ecosystems.

The success of organisations in a world of digitalisation and increasing global competition ultimately lies in their ability to continuously and flexibly adapt their DNA, i.e. the organisational structures and business processes. Breaking down silos and fostering collaboration enables organisations to effectively leverage their resources, skills and capabilities to drive growth and keep pace with technological development.

The success of organisations lies in their ability to continuously adapt their business processes.

When used correctly, technologies such as business and process intelligence tools provide valuable insights that enable organisations to quickly and accurately identify areas for improvement and make data-driven decisions.

However, all of this is associated with fundamental changes, and change requires strong leadership, determination and resilience because change is always a counter-movement to rigid and existing systems and structures that vehemently resist change. As long as such changes are not driven forward holistically and with a strong will, there is a risk that the existing structures will swallow them up over time. This does not mean you cannot start small, nor do you have to implement new approaches with a big bang effect or via the back door. But it means that without a holistic approach and the courage to tackle manifested realities and structures, many endeavours will fail, or such initiatives will be on the verge of burnout.

In this book, we highlight organisational aspects of an entrepreneurial organisation that go beyond pure process management but are essential for achieving process excellence. With this book, let's build the 'Process Excellence Enterprise' and examine the necessary aspects for efficient and effective process reengineering or organisational transformation.

> **_'The truth is rarely pure and never simple.'_**
>
> _- Oscar Wilde -_

1. From **complexity to 'digital' transformation**

A spaceship⬛🔹is **complex** because it comprises many interconnected components, systems, and processes. The complexity results from the multidimensional relationships and interactions between these elements. For example, a spaceship has advanced propulsion systems, life support systems, navigation systems, communication systems, and much more. Each of these systems requires a high level of expertise to operate. This complexity is then increased by the fact that all these highly specialised systems communicate with each other in networks and have interrelationships.

Furthermore, countless details **complicate** the spaceship if the underlying principles and interrelationships are not sufficiently understood. The complicated aspects of a spaceship can include the design of the individual components, specific and defined operation procedures, and the crew's organisational structure. These make the management of the spaceship more difficult if responsibilities are unclear and too fragmented in detail or remain in encrusted structures.

Complexity as a driver of change and transformation

The term complexity is generally used to describe the dimensionality, degree of difficulty, level of expertise or effort required to understand a system, problem, concept, process or situation. Complexity can also be quantified by factors such as the number of elements, the connections between them, the degree of uncertainty or unpredictability and the amount of information or data involved. Complexity occurs in various fields, e.g., mathematics, biology, sociology, and everyday life situations. Managing complexity consists of breaking down the whole into smaller, more manageable parts, understanding their relationships and interactions, and developing strategies to understand, control and/or solve problems within the complex system.

More than ever, complexity will drive change and transformation because as systems, technologies, regulations and organisations become more complex, they will encounter challenges that can no longer be overcome with traditional structures, methods, competencies and skills. Uncontrolled, complex environments lead to inefficiencies, communication barriers and difficulties if they are not addressed proactively. To navigate and evolve in the 'new' complexity, organisations often need to make fundamental changes, introduce structural innovations and redesign their structures and processes to remain effective and competitive.

The increasing complexity of organisations

Organisations are complex ecosystems comprising various interconnected components, such as locations, departments, teams, processes, technologies, data, regulations, expertise, languages, cultures and people. These components all interact with each other daily on multidimensional levels and influence an organisation's overall functioning and culture.

For various reasons, this will become even more acute in the future:

🜂 **Globalisation:** As organisations expand their operations geographically, they have to deal with different languages and cultures, flows of goods and market dynamics.

♠ Technological progress: The rapid pace of technological progress introduces new tools, platforms and systems into organisations that must be integrated and managed.

♠ Further specialisation with simultaneous diversification: Organisations specialise <u>and</u> diversify to make their product portfolio even broader and more customer-oriented, thus meeting the requirements of different markets.

♠ Changing market and customer expectations: With increasing digitalisation, customers expect personalised and seamless experiences just in time. Organisations need to operate a new (digital) form of customer relationship management to fulfil these expectations.

♠ Regulatory and compliance requirements: Organisations must comply with a growing number of laws, standards, and other regulations that vary from market to market and require sophisticated reporting, extensive control systems, and documentation.

♠ Mergers and acquisitions: To speed up competition, mergers and acquisitions will continue to increase, which requires an equally rapid integration of different languages, cultures, systems, processes, and data.

All these factors and more turn organisations into highly complex ecosystems. But please let us differentiate between complex and complicated at this point. Different measures are required to transform organisations and processes depending on whether something is complex or complicated.

When complexity becomes complicated

The terms 'complex' and 'complicated' are often used inter-changeably but have different meanings and effects.

'Complex' is something that, by nature, consists of various interconnected and interrelated parts or elements. It shows a high degree of complexity or sophistication when a more pro-found understanding or analysis is required to understand an issue thoroughly. However, complex systems can be well structured, organised and predictable once the underlying principles are understood.

On the other hand, 'complicated' refers to something difficult to understand or manage due to its intricacy or the multitude of factors that are not necessarily interdependent. It implies a higher degree of difficulty, making tasks or situations more difficult to manage. Complicated systems often require more clarity and are more difficult to understand. Examples of com-plicated scenarios are bureaucratic processes, evolved traffic infrastructures in large cities or intertwined legal systems.

In short, **complexity is** in the nature of things and **complica-ted** is what we humans often make of it. The challenge in today's orga-nisational life is that many organisa-tions are a mixture of both, and dis-tinguishing between complex and complicated situations will become essential for any organisation's fu-ture success. Complexity needs to be understood and mana-ged, and complicated situations, by contrast, must be reco-gnised, eliminated or simplified. So, what do we find if we

Complexity is in the nature of things and complicated is what we humans often make of it.

take a hard look inside our organisations? Complex structures and processes, or complicated structures and processes, or both? And what role does this distinction play in digitalisation? Shouldn't we first simplify complicated structures and processes and master complex structures and processes before we digitalise them?

The complexity of the 'digital' transformation

'Digital transformation' is the number one buzzword in almost all industries. But what does it mean? After all, digitalisation is not really new and has been practised for decades.

Reduced to the lowest common denominator, digitalisation refers to converting analogue information into digital formats that can be processed electronically and thus offer new possibilities for use. It is about using digital tools and platforms to stabilise, accelerate and optimise processes. This, in turn, aims to improve efficiency and effectiveness, open up new business models, enhance the customer experience and remain competitive in today's fast-paced and technology-driven world.

The digital transformation includes:

🔥 **Technology integration:** Adopting and integrating new technologies such as cloud computing, artificial intelligence, Internet of Things (IoT), big data analytics, automation and machine learning into existing systems and processes.

🔥 **Process optimisation:** Analysis and redesign of business processes to eliminate redundant steps, minimise manual intervention, reduce complexity, leverage digital technologies and improve overall efficiency and productivity.

🔥 **Customer centricity:** Focus on delivering exceptional customer experiences through the use of digital channels, personalisation and seamless customer experiences across multiple touchpoints.

🔥 **Data-driven insights:** Collecting, analysing and using data to gain valuable insights, drive decision-making, identify trends, predict customer behaviour and develop new business models.

🔥 **Agile culture:** Includes fast and innovative adaptability and continuous improvement. It promotes cross-functional collaboration, transparency, personal responsibility, quick decision-making, and adaptability to changing customer and market requirements.

🔥 **Organisational change:** Promoting a culture of change and continuous learning, training or retraining the workforce, forming cross-functional teams and defining new roles and responsibilities to facilitate the 'digital' transformation.

The ultimate goal of 'digital' transformation is to enable organisations to harness and improve the power of digital technologies to drive new business models and growth, increase competitiveness and create sustainable value in an increasingly digital and connected world.

'Digitisation' is not the same as 'digitalisation'[1]

'Digitisation' and 'digitalisation' are integral parts of the broader concept of digital transformation. Digital transformation is the application of digital technologies to fundamentally change an organisation's operations, business models and strategies to adapt to changing market conditions and meet the demands of the

'Digitisation' is the process of converting analogue data into digital data. 'Digitalisation' is the strategic use of digitised data and digital technologies.

digital age. But what is the difference between 'digitisation' and 'digitalisation', and why is it important to distinguish between them?

Digitisation involves converting analogue or physical data into digital formats. This process ensures that the data is accessible electronically, a fundamental prerequisite for the effective use of digital technologies. On the path to 'digital' transformation, digitised and structured data forms the basis for advanced analyses, machine learning, and data-driven decisions.

Digitalisation is made possible by 'digitisation'. In this advanced phase, digitised data and digital technologies are used to redesign and optimise business processes, improve the customer experience and drive innovation. Here, organisations use digital data and technologies to develop further and optimise their processes. This includes the integrative con-

---

[1] In German, there is no distinction between 'digitisation' and 'digitalisation'. Both are referred to as digitalisation. Perhaps this linguistic subtlety explains why digitalisation is so stagnant in the German-speaking world.

nectivity of different technologies, the automation of tasks, the improvement of data analysis and the improvement of communication and collaboration. Digitalisation aims to remain competitive in a rapidly evolving digital landscape by using the opportunities offered by technology in a customer- and business-oriented manner.

The development of the 'digital' transformation

The aspects mentioned above lead to different phases or levels organisations go through when implementing digital technologies to improve their processes and business models. Each level builds on the previous level. The complexity of 'digital' transformation is often complicated because organisations are at different maturity levels, both as a whole and internally, between departments, divisions and/or locations. But let's first take a look at the individual levels in detail[2] :

1st foundation level: The foundation serves as the pyramid's base and focuses on creating the necessary infrastructure to support the 'digital' transformation. This includes investments in robust IT systems, reliable network infrastructure and appropriate data storage and security measures. With a solid foundation, it is easier for organisations to implement digital solutions and adapt effectively to rapid technological progress.

2nd utilisation layer: The utilisation layer is the middle level of the pyramid and comprises the use of digital technologies to

---

[2] Gupta, M. Sen What is Digitization, Digitalization, and Digital Transformation-Clarifying Terminology. Available online: https://www.arcweb.com/blog/what-digitization-digitalization-digital-transformation
(accessed on 2 March 2024).

further improve existing business processes and workflows. This layer focuses on automation, data analysis, artificial intelligence and machine learning. Organisations at this level try to optimise their processes through further system-side networking and integration, improve efficiency and gain valuable insights from data to make better decisions with data-based information.

3rd innovation level: The innovation level represents the top of the pyramid and is characterised by organisations fully embracing digital transformation. At this level, organisations utilise emerging technologies such as virtual reality, blockchain and advanced analytics to develop innovative products, services and business models. The main focus here is staying one step ahead of the competition and driving continuous innovation to create new customer value.

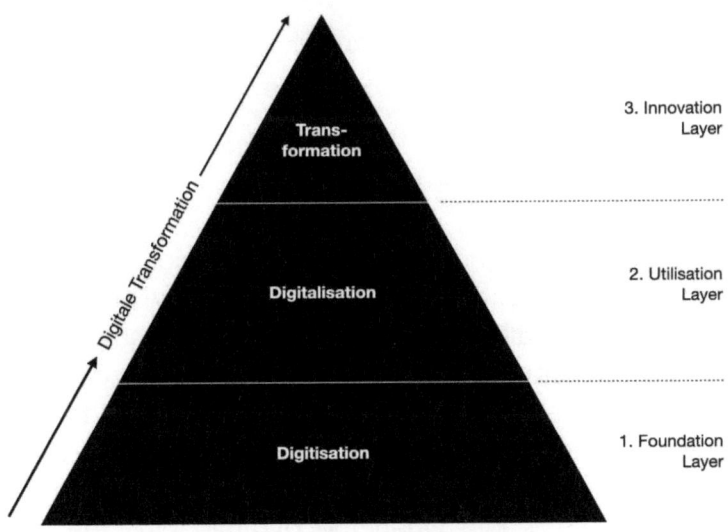

1. **Pyramid of 'digital' transformation: from foundation to innovation**

It is important to note that the pyramid of 'digital' transformation (see Figure 1) is not strictly linear, i.e. organisations can work on several levels simultaneously. However, moving up the pyramid as a whole requires significant investment in technologies, skills, and competencies, as well as understanding the end-to-end process and a massive cultural shift towards 'digital' transformation. By understanding this framework, organisations can better plan and strategise their 'digital' transformation journey by assessing where they are!

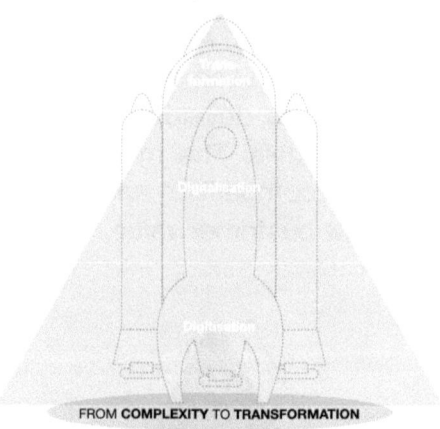

FROM **COMPLEXITY** TO **TRANSFORMATION**

2. Process Excellence Enterprise

The third level is the most popular because it is the most exciting and attractive. This is undoubtedly one reason why around 70% of all digital transformation projects in all industries fail. So don't underestimate the importance of the first two levels, even if they are less sexy. They fuel the 'Process Excellence Enterprise' (see Figure 2) and will give your innovation journey an enormous boost on the third level. The journey can, therefore, begin when the pyramid plus the difference between complicated and complex is considered.

Take away

Complex and complicated are two different terms. Complexity arises naturally and requires a deeper understanding, while complicated situations result from human-made entanglements. Organisations must distinguish between these two terms, as dealing with complexity requires understanding and management, while complicated situations must be recognised, simplified, or eliminated.

Digital transformation encompasses both 'digitisation' (converting analogue data into digital) and 'digitalisation' (strategic use of digital data and technologies to improve processes and customer experience) to adapt to the digital age and remain competitive. Digital transformation occurs across several levels, with the third level often receiving the most attention. However, the first two levels, which include investments in technology and cultural change, form the basis as drivers **Neglecting the first two levels will massively hinder innovation and lead to a crashing failure.** for innovations in the third level. Neglecting the first two levels, including additional complicated organisational structures, will massively hinder innovation and lead to a crashing failure. In turn, understanding this framework helps organisations to plan and design their 'digital' transformation effectively.

In summary, a successful digital transformation requires an assessment of the current status quo, an end-to-end understanding of processes, and a strategic approach with investments in digital technologies and cultural change towards increased acceptance (**and is, therefore, not just a 'digital'**

transformation!). If implemented correctly, this will lead to higher efficiency, flexibility and a better customer experience.

But what if the assessment reveals that data and processes are based on outdated hierarchies, systems and infrastructures and are just rubbish? Or, to put it another way: would you dare to travel through the galaxy if your navigation data came from different legacy systems in various formats and these were thrown together to steer your spaceship? This recognition takes courage in many organisations, as it will show the difference between desire and reality. It requires an investment in fundamental reengineering of structures and processes before one can even begin to speak of a 'digital' transformation. This is often overlooked and is probably another reason why more than three-quarters of 'digital' transformation initiatives fail mercilessly.

> *'Insanity is doing the same thing over and over again and expecting different results.'*
>
> *- Albert Einstein -*

2. From **enterprise capabilities** to **organisational structures**

Imagine the 🚀 *spaceship Enterprise hurtling through the infinite expanse of space while its crew swarm around like caffeinated squirrels. The crew is equipped with the traditional structures and skills, i.e. the space explorer Jimmy at the helm, who is always defeated by his ego, the engineer Freddy with his hamster wheel drive, the navigator Nelly with her talent for getting lost in details, the communications professional Carl with his social media powers and the doctor Mandy who diagnoses a monster rash from every mosquito bite. The crew is highly motivated, and the spaceship Enterprise is ready for a wild ride. No matter where they end up, the flight will be entertaining!*

Once a harmonious team, the crew was caught in a complicated web that had increased over the years due to upgrades and modifications. The more difficulties arose, the more each member tried to find individual solutions. But most solutions led to new, unforeseen challenges and problems. The navigation team, dazzled by their advanced star chart instruments, overlooked their impact on the overloaded power grid. At the same time, the development team implemented one new add-on after another in the pursuit of greater efficiency because technical solutions were the panacea for all problems. Looking at the Enterprise from the outside, it was like being in a buzzing ant's nest, with all crew members busily working on enhancements. As time passed, however, exhaustion set in, and the calls for more crew members grew louder and louder. The crew members were 'suddenly' dealing with interdisciplinary contexts and structures that were difficult to master, but wasn't this a gradual process, and didn't it require more players and skills beyond the traditional core competencies?

In many organisations, rapid growth or growth, in general, has meant that not enough attention has been paid to adapting structures, processes and skills because - and perhaps with good reason - capacities and resources have been used for other priorities or because it was simply not foreseeable what changes growth, globalisation and increased regulation would bring. Or perhaps it was merely assumed that everything would continue linearly and that the old and traditional strengths would continue to be sufficient for the future. In the end, of course, this is just speculation and doesn't matter because the fact that organisations have to change fundamentally is no longer disputed. The question now is, how must an organisation change, and how do we take everyone on this journey?

The development of the spaceship Enterprise described above can be perceived as wild, uncoordinated or chaotic. However, this is not because of a lack of motivation but because there is a lack of essential capabilities for transformation. The transformation of organisations requires new enterprise capabilities, not only because existing enterprise capabilities have evolved but also because new enterprise capabilities, such as managing complexity, are needed.

The illusion that new technologies will standardise and harmonise processes is promoted by many software providers.

Many software providers take advantage of this and propagate the illusion that new technologies will standardise and harmonise existing structures and processes. This overlooks the fact that most organisations are complex and complicated ecosystems. Furthermore, the highly interconnected nature of today's business environment means that organisations must navigate a web of internal and external relationships. Global supply chains and markets, diverse teams in different cultures and complex legal and technical frameworks all contribute to the complex network of modern organisations. At the same time, the increasing speed of change requires organisations to become more agile and adaptable.

In essence, managing complexity is a new enterprise capability because the demands on the business management of organisations go far beyond traditional approaches and behaviours. It is not just about managing complexity but also about utilising it strategically and conceptually. Organisations that master this capability can turn complexity into a competitive advantage, driving innovation, resilience and sustainable success in an increasingly complex business world. Without this capability, chaos will ensue, leading to a wild and uncontrolled journey. This, in turn, will lead to a waste of intellectual and material resources as well as misunderstandings and conflicts between team members. In other words, without sophisticated management of the transformation process with new enterprise capabilities, there will be a lack of accountability and direction. Responsibilities and functions will have their own goals and priorities, making aligning efforts and achieving the desired outcome difficult. This inevitably leads to inefficiencies, delays, or even blockages, ultimately resulting in the desired goals not being achieved or the entire organisation's success being jeopardised.

Assessment of enterprise capabilities as a business enabler

Enterprise capabilities are the skills, resources and competencies an organisation must have to achieve its strategic goals effectively and efficiently. Enterprise capabilities describe the 'WHAT', i.e. what an organisation must do and have to deliver products and/or services and compete in the market. In the past, depending on the business model, traditional skills such as finance, production, logistics, sales, marketing, service, development, and research were the centre of attention and naturally retained their importance. But they are no longer nearly enough. In the context of 'digital' transformation, it is crucial to understand that new capabilities in the context of managing complexity, such as information security management, disaster recovery, business (BI) and process intelligence (PI), (agile) business process reengineering, information architecture management (EAM), (master) data management, (enterprise) risk management, compliance, etc. are necessary or need to be prioritised and developed. Given this, if organisations want to remain or become efficient, effective and scalable, it is essential to radically review and reassess the current enterprise capabilities of an organisation concerning current and future requirements.

Capability maturity models as your basis

Maturity models can be used as a reference for carrying out and analysing the capabilities of an organisation. These provide a sound basis, structure and suggestions for a comprehensive assessment. There are various maturity models. The Capability Maturity Model Integration (CMMI) is one of the best-known models. The CMMI is particularly suitable for organisations that develop or purchase software, systems and/

or hardware. It also supports the improvement of organisations that provide services. What is unique about the CMMI model is that it not only highlights technical skills but also addresses the supporting skills of the organisation, such as resource planning, process management, and employee empowerment.

Other maturity models include the Agile Capability Model (ACM), the DevOps Capability Model (DCMM), Capability-based Software Development (CBSD) and SAFe (Scaled Agile Framework), all of which have their justification and were developed to solve specific problems. The choice of the suitable model depends on the particular goals, size, business model and industry.

Enterprise capabilities as a prerequisite for change

When an organisation (re)develops or renews its strategy, it needs to reassess and redefine its enterprise capabilities to align them with potential new objectives and close any capability gaps. This process enables organisations to adapt to market changes, effectively manage potential risks and strive for efficiency by eliminating redundancies and fostering a culture focused on innovation and learning. In this context, assessing organisational capabilities is not a one-time event. It must be carried out continuously to flexibly support and drive the strategy and corporate objectives. The assessment of enterprise capabilities aims to identify missing enterprise capabilities and examine the effectiveness of existing enterprise capabilities and how they are distributed or grouped within an organisation. Based on this, we identify and assess the enterprise's capabilities and determine the required resources and capacities for new or changed capabilities. We also evaluate whether investing in resources, technology, and/or labour skills is necessary. The organisational structure of roles, job positions, responsibilities, and reporting lines is also analysed. Depending on the results, this may mean that the (target) operating model (TOM) needs to be adapted or reorganised.

The following will focus on the enterprise capabilities associated with constant change and increasing complexity. These need to be examined more thoroughly than ever to prepare an organisation for future challenges and requirements in the face of exponentially increasing complexity.

- **Business process management and reengineering:** Implementation of BPM[3] principles and methods for structuring and visualising end-to-end processes, minimising waste, optimising resources and streamlining workflows, leading to a better understanding of complexity and thus to cost savings and improved efficiency.

- **Agile project management:** Introduction of agile methods for continuous, iterative, more flexible and customer-orientated development of products, services, structures and processes.

- **Quality control and assurance:** Ensuring that products and services meet or exceed the specified quality standards and that quality is continuously monitored and improved.

- **Change management:** Effective management of personnel, as well as structural and procedural changes, to ensure a smooth transition.

---

[3] Business Process Management

- **Data Science/Analytics and Business/Process Intelligence:** Using data analytics and business/process intelligence tools to make data-driven decisions and gain insights into business performance and customer behaviour.

- **Management of regulations:** Ensuring that the organisation complies with the relevant laws and regulations, industry-specific standards, and internal guidelines.

- **Risk management:** Identification, assessment and mitigation of business risks that threaten the existence of an organisation's activities and objectives.

- **Cyber security and data protection:** developing robust procedures to protect sensitive data and ensure the security of an organisation's digital assets.

- **Performance management:** Definition and measurement of processes and key performance indicators to track and evaluate the effectiveness of various processes and functions.

- **Strategy and project portfolio management:** Strategic management of projects to ensure alignment with corporate goals, prioritise resources in a focused manner and optimise project results.

- **Knowledge management:** Recording, organising and passing on knowledge within the organisation to transfer knowledge across functions, facilitate well-founded decisions and promote innovation.

- **Organisational and employee development:** Continuous adaptation of structural and procedural organisations and

implementation of continuous training and skills development processes to improve the performance and adaptability of employees.

These cross-functional enterprise capabilities, extending beyond traditional product and service-related capabilities, are
crucial for organisations to adapt, compete, and thrive in the
modern business world. It is not just a question of whether an
organisation has these enterprise capabilities but rather how
they are developed in relation to the business objectives.

Not to be forgotten, of course, are the so-called social and
emotional skills, such as adaptability, collaboration, leadership, creativity, critical and entrepreneurial thinking, communication and networking, personal responsibility, cooperation, cultural awareness, customer orientation, stress management, conflict resolution and the ability to work remotely,
which also contribute to the organisation's success and need
to be organised and continuously developed, but are not considered further at this point.

Take Away

In earlier times, once-defined enterprise capabilities survived
for a long time. In recent decades, however, enterprise capabilities have changed significantly, and new enterprise capabilities are not only hugely important for the success of organisations but also essential for survival. In our increasingly fast-
moving world, it is necessary to regularly review the expectations and requirements of organisations. This is about more
than just whether or not an enterprise capability exists but
also the capacity and extent to which it supports the organisation's objectives. Otherwise, there is a risk that investments
in new business models and newly introduced technologies

will not pay off or even become a cost burden. Traditional enterprise capabilities and change mechanisms are no longer sufficient, and fundamental transformations with new enterprise capabilities have become necessary.

For example, the development from the carriage to the automobile took a comparatively long time compared to today's technological developments. In intermediate phases, steam engines were installed in carriages. This is similar to traditional mechanisms of evolutionary development and adaptation, but it was not a transformation and certainly occurred because technological developments took much longer than 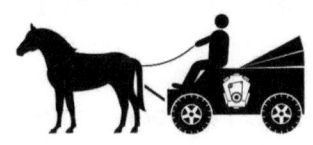 they do today. Years later, further adaptations and developments led to the invention of the internal combustion engine and the first automobiles. The leap from the carriage to the car would have been a transformation, but it was more or less a continuous development (change). Today's technological developments are much more rapid and exponential. So, suppose organisations want to stay at the forefront of their mar-

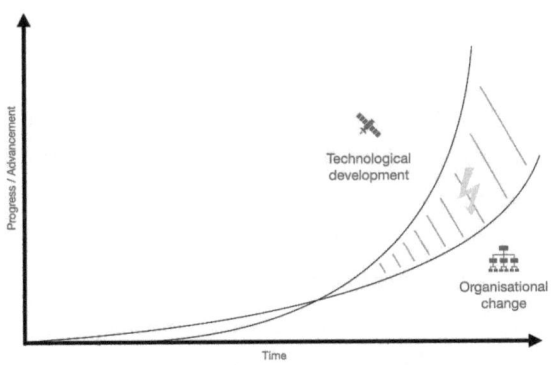

3. Technological development vs. organisational development

kets. In that case, they must adapt their enterprise capabilities to the new technological requirements to keep pace with technological developments. If this is not achieved quickly and appropriately, organisations risk increasing divergence between technological and organisational developments. (see Figure 3). In these cases, metaphorically speaking, organisations will continue to install steam engines and racing tyres on the chassis of the carriage.

Decoding organisational structures

In the galaxy's vastness, our spaceship *Enterprise embarked on a monumental expedition fuelled by pure ambition and cutting-edge technology. The individual crew members recognised the change and redefined their capabilities. However, the deeper the crew ventured into unexplored space, the more apparent the lack of coherent structures became, as the new capabilities led to overlapping responsibilities, creating turbulence between team members. This was exacerbated because different systems were increasingly clashing and were not synchronised. Without a holistic plan, the propulsion system was now fighting against the navigation control system, which led to inefficiencies in flight behaviour and risked critical errors.*

Amid the cosmic voyage, unforeseen challenges emerged that caught the crew off guard. Resource allocation became unpredictable, leading to shortages in critical areas and overcapacity in others, increasingly impacting the ship's ability to function. The more problems arose, the more human resources were requested. Everyone was eager and motivated at work. A lot of overtime was put in, but the more they worked, the worse it became. But what was the problem, or what was still missing? Was the team on the right track to define the new enterprise capabilities?

An organisational structure describes the framework and hierarchy that defines an organisation and how the various enterprise capabilities, roles, positions, and responsibilities are distributed among its members. It also outlines the organisation's relationships, communication channels, and decision-making processes.

Traditional organisational structures are often designed based on specific organisational functions or departments. These structures group employees based on their specific skills and specialisms. In particular, departments such as finance, marketing, logistics, production, and human resources are usually separate units within the organisation.

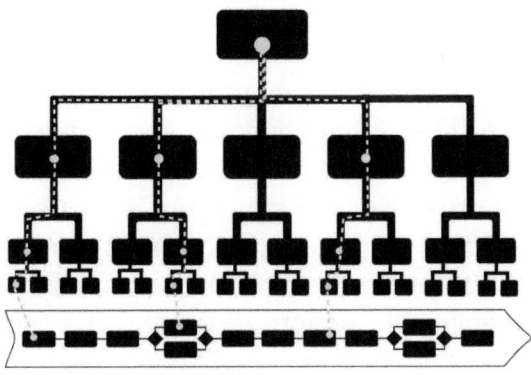

4. Decision-making processes in a functional organisational structure

Functional organisational structures are simple because they are easy to implement. An organisation is broken down into specialist parts (skills), and a simple top-down and bottom-up communication and hierarchy structure can also be set up comparatively 'quickly'.

But the disadvantages are also apparent. What if two or more middle or lower-hierarchical-level specialists have to coordinate and make decisions? Such a structure means long vertical zigzag decision paths (see Figure 4). In addition, such decision paths are often like whispering mail, and decisions made at the top of an organisation are frequently based on interpretation rather than hard facts and information. Similarly, such decision-making processes usually take far too long.

In the future, enterprise capabilities such as process intelligence will emerge or be further developed that cannot be assigned to just one functional unit. However, what impact will this have on a functional organisational structure if similar or identical skills are required in different areas? In such cases, how can it be ensured that such distributed capabilities are coordinated and organised to avoid unnecessary friction and redundancies? For this reason, among others, organisations need to rethink their organisational structures and transform towards more flexible, interconnected and dynamic structures to foster better integration and collaboration between silos. This change in organisational structures is a rollercoaster ride of emotions because it is a paradigm shift compared to the way of working of the last century, and such massive changes require the opening of comfort zones and the breakdown of encrusted established departmental boundaries.

Of course, there are several possible future organisational structures in addition to the traditional functional organisational structures, and some of them address the challenges of the problems mentioned above well. However, despite these challenges, there is no ideal blueprint for an organisation; each must find its own model and adapt it to its needs.

Here are some possible alternatives at a glance (without claiming to be complete):

Matrix organisational structure

Advantages:

🔔 Enables efficient resource allocation and utilisation

🔔 Improves cross-functional collaboration and communication

🔔 Enables flexibility and adaptability to changing circumstances

Disadvantages:

🔔 This can lead to power struggles and conflicts between functional and cross-functional managers (e.g. project or process managers)

🔔 This can lead to confusion and complexity due to dual reporting lines

🔔 Requires strong leadership, coordination and communication skills

Network organisational structure

Advantages:

🔔 Facilitates collaboration and knowledge sharing between different organisations

🔔 Provides access to specialised skills and resources from various partners

🔔 Enables flexibility and scalability

Disadvantages:

🔥 Management can be difficult due to the involvement of numerous stakeholders

🔥 Requires effective coordination and communication mechanisms

🔥 This can lead to less control and accountability

Agile organisational structure

Advantages:

🔥 Enables quick decision-making and response to customer needs

🔥 Improves collaboration and self-organisation in teams

🔥 Promotes a culture of continuous learning and improvement

Disadvantages:

🔥 Requires a high level of maturity and can be challenging to implement in larger organisations

🔥 Requires strong leadership through objectives and management support

🔥 This can lead to more complexity and coordination effort

Flat organisational structure

Advantages:

🔥 Promotes a culture of openness and transparency

🔥 Facilitates faster decision-making and communication

🔥 Fosters employee commitment and personal responsibility

Disadvantages:

🔥 This can lead to unclear allocation of roles and a lack of a clear hierarchy

🔥 This can lead to increased workload and stress for employees

🔥 Requires strong leadership and communication skills

Process-orientated structure

Advantages:

🔥 Transparent processes promote efficiency through a structured approach

🔥 Process-oriented processes facilitate communication and collaboration within the organisation

🔥 With the help of process performance indicators (PPI), organisations can track their performance and make data-driven decisions.

Disadvantages:

🔥 Employees can resist changes to established processes

🔥 Overemphasising processes can lead to rigidity

🔥 If the process documentation needs to be clarified or updated, this can lead to misunderstandings and errors.

Many organisations have recognised that their structures must adapt to the new framework conditions. But what happens when the project management office demands and promotes an **agile organisation** and culture, marketing management tries to establish a **network organisation**, process management introduces **process structures** and/or a **matrix organisation**, and department heads, managers, and specialists stick to their **functional structures**? As if it were not challenging enough to change a functional organisation in just one direction, different new organisational models are often driven forward in parallel in organisations without coordination. This is done with goodwill and intentions. However, it increases change management exponentially, throws even more sand into the gears, and can slow down an organisation instead of making it more efficient and effective.

Furthermore, organisations like to follow new socio-psychological approaches that demand more individual responsibility and joint decision-making. However, the desired target state and the reality are often far apart. Does an organisation have the communication skills required for a matrix organisation, or does it have the skills to implement process-oriented structures? Are organisations with decades or even centuries of conventional DNA ready for transparency, autonomous decision-making and collaboration in cross-functional teams, or what is needed to get them there?

This is precisely why assessing the current state is essential to derive suitable measures from the mismatch between the current and target state. This assessment must also consider the history of the organisations and what has made them so strong, as the success of most organisations has its reasons and was very compatible with the existing structures in the past.

A new organisational structure can only be implemented with the necessary skills, which must be developed and/or expanded. It is only possible to implement a new organisational structure efficiently with the essential new enterprise capabilities. However, developing a new enterprise capability requires its application in a corresponding organisational structure. A great deal of sensitivity is required from organisations to implement this simultaneously and in a balanced manner because what is needed first? The chicken (new organisational structure) or the egg (new enterprise capabilities)? This is one of the reasons why organisations find restructuring so extremely difficult and often fail. It also means that new processes, roles, responsibilities, and possibly new technologies must be established and implemented with the change or adaptation of new enterprise capabilities and integrated into the enterprise strategy and objectives. In this context, integrating organisational development with strong change management skills and an elementary enterprise capability that is ideally already professionally developed is necessary. It is imperative to adequately carry out and provide qualification measures and adjustments to employee structures, job descriptions, roles, titles, and authorisations.

In this context, an organisation's culture that has grown over the years should be considered, as it can hinder new organisational structures. The saying goes: 'Culture not only eats strategy but also (new) structures for breakfast.' Therefore, assessing change management skills must also be considered and should not be underestimated, especially in organisations with encrusted structures.

Culture not only eats strategy but also (new) structures for breakfast.

The suitability and adaptability of an organisational structure or model depends on various factors, such as the industry, the size of the organisation, its specific objectives and culture. Organisations can adopt hybrid structures and combine elements from different models to best suit their needs and circumstances.

For change management reasons, it is also essential to orchestrate organisational change top-down and bring together the stakeholders who are working on various structural changes (usually simultaneously, e.g. agility, project management, digitalisation, process and data orientation, etc.) to eliminate redundancies in the definition of skills, roles and responsibilities and establish uniform procedures and processes across the organisation. Ultimately, it is advisable to bring together precisely those stakeholders who are driving the introduction of such new concepts and structures from different perspectives and needs to prevent the formation of additional cross-functional silos. Otherwise, the silos will not be broken down, but we will refurbish and modify old functional structures.

Here is a list of essential factors that are absolutely necessary:

- **Clear objectives**: Clearly defined objectives and reasons for change must ensure that the new structure aligns with the organisation's goals and vision.

- **Management support:** Strong management support is essential to effectively drive and implement change. Managers must communicate the need for change, provide guidance, and accompany and monitor the transition process.

- **Involvement of interest groups:** The participation of key stakeholders is necessary to gain support and harness synergies. Their input can also help to design a structure that meets multiple needs.

- **Communication strategy**: A well-planned communication strategy is essential to inform all stakeholders about the change, its purpose, and its benefits. Transparent, consistent, and continuous communication helps manage expectations and reduce uncertainty.

🚀 **Resources and qualifications**: Adequate resources, including financial, technological, and human resources, are required to implement the new structure successfully. Ensuring that employees have the necessary skills and training to adapt to it is also essential.

🚀 **Change management plan**: A comprehensive change management plan must define the steps, timeline, and responsibilities to implement the new structure. This plan should address potential challenges and include strategies to mitigate resistance.

🚀 **Evaluation and feedback**: Regular evaluation and feedback mechanisms are necessary to assess the effectiveness of the new structure and make the required adjustments. This allows the organisation to continuously improve and adapt to changing circumstances.

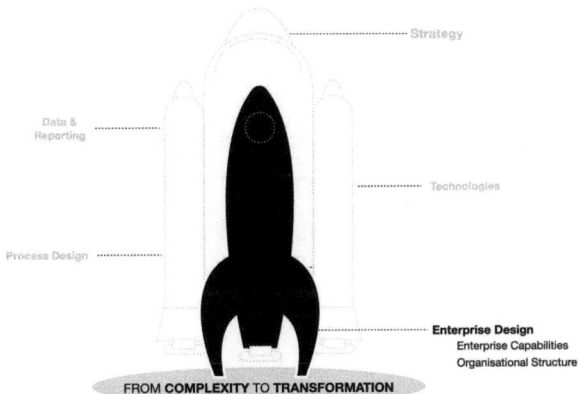

5. **Process Excellence Enterprise: From enterprise capabilities to organisational structures**

A combination of these factors is imperative to successfully change an organisational structure. Each organisation may have specific requirements and considerations, but taking these critical elements into account increases the likelihood of a smooth transition to new, innovative, or hybrid structures and is the basis for a 'Process Excellence Enterprise' (see Figure 5).

In summary, a change or transformation of the organisational structure usually also entails changes to the organisation's capabilities and culture. As one cannot be developed without the other and there are interdependencies, these must be developed simultaneously and dynamically. Changing organisational structures is, therefore, a mammoth task, as it means developing new enterprise capabilities, which organisations must acquire through empowerment or acquisition, and changing the culture through change management measures as well as an appropriate communication strategy and the management of various interest groups with different perspectives and parallel concepts. This is, of course, a tightrope act and, if inadequately orchestrated, leads organisations to the brink of madness.

> *'Education is the most powerful weapon you can use to change the world.'*
>
> *- Nelson Mandela -*

3. From **roles** to smart **processes**

Facilitating cross-functional collaboration, especially in functional organisational structures, with clear responsibilities is another building block for the efficient transformation of organisations. This is all the more true as many organisations with functional structures have not yet recognised the extent of waste caused by redundancies and incongruities between functional silos. Employees from different functional areas unknowingly work on the same tasks in parallel, and processes are unknowingly and happily 'optimised' and complicated redundantly. Defining clear roles is essential to improving cross-functional collaboration and ensuring process excellence. By defining task and process-related responsibilities of individual team members, potential conflicts and ambiguities can be avoided. So, if you want your teams to achieve exceptional results, you should define clear roles and responsibilities from the outset. Roles help to define transparent workflows between functions that support specialisation depending on the process, streamline processes and create hierarchies and decision-making paths that contribute to overall operational efficiency.

The difference between roles and job positions

Roles and job positions are related concepts but have different meanings. A role refers to a set of responsibilities, tasks, and expectations assigned to an individual within an organisation or group. It defines the specific functions and tasks a person must perform to achieve the organisation's goals. Roles can be broad or specific, often requiring certain skills and competencies assigned to particular tasks and procedures.

On the other hand, a job position refers to a specific employment opportunity and a job title within the organisational hierarchy. It is, therefore, the formal identification of a person's place within the organisational structure. Job positions are often associated with specific authorisations and reporting lines. It is a more general term that encompasses the tasks and responsibilities associated with multiple roles.

While job positions are more formal and hierarchical, roles tend to focus on the tasks and responsibilities the person in question fulfils. Depending on the organisation's needs and requirements, individuals may sometimes hold multiple roles within a single job position. Understanding the difference between roles and job positions is critical to the effective organisation and allocation of work in the process organisation.

Clear and well-defined roles will be more critical than ever in the future. In contrast to a purely functional organisation, the increasing complexity resulting from regulation, globalisation and digitalisation requires cross-functional teams with the necessary skills to solve extensive and multidimensional situations. This is particularly true when functional organisational structures are transformed into more modern (hybrid) ones, as this is the only way to ensure and promote networking (e.g., matrix and process-oriented structures) and collaboration. For example, specific marketing, sales or purchasing employees can be appointed to the role of process analyst or expert as an additional part of their traditional and day-to-day tasks and procedures. In this role, these individuals also work with colleagues in cross-functional teams to analyse and improve the business process. In addition to their traditional tasks, employees take on additional roles in different structures that require new competencies. In this way, roles help to establish more precise responsibilities and relationships within the organisation and thus actively tackle the complexity of an eco-system.

Roles as a binding agent for cooperation and collaboration

The key skills and resources required to successfully meet expectations and objectives are identified by analysing and evaluating an organisation's enterprise capabilities. As already mentioned, these capabilities are allocated to specific roles and functions. In particular, data analysis skills can be utilised in roles such as Data Scientist or Process Intelligence Analyst. In contrast, leadership and change management skills can be implemented in roles such as Team Manager, Project Manager, Process Manager and Process Owner. Assigning skills to roles ensures that the organisation's employees are structured, equipped and positioned in such a way that they can achieve the strategic goals. Skills serve as building blocks that enable individuals to fulfil their tasks effectively and contribute to the joint success of the organisation. This will be particularly important in the future, as the traditional education programmes of many professions do not yet include the crucial skills to master complexity. Organisations must, therefore, recognise these gaps and set up appropriate training programmes. This focus will promote efficiency, effectiveness, specialisation, collaboration, better resource allocation, innovation and agility.

But be careful because if the role definition is not centrally controlled and orchestrated, it can have the opposite effect. The importance of roles is recognised in many organisations. Still, in many places, this leads to role inflation as individual functional units start to invent their roles within their silos. This is particularly risky for roles with cross-functional capabilities as it will lead to devastating redundancies and new frictions. **Agile Coaches, Scrum Masters, Product Owners, Project Managers, Project Portfolio Managers, Process Owners, Process Managers, Digital Transformation Officers, Process Improvement Managers, Subject Matter Experts, Key Users, Process Experts, Process Coordinators, Process Automation Officers, Business Analysts, Data Analysts, Data Engineers, Data Scientists, Data Stewards, Process Analysts, Risk Owners, Risk Managers, Metric Owners, Metric Developers, Report Owners, Data Owners, Application Owners, Citizen Developers, Process Architects, Enterprise Architects, Solution Architects, Business Partners, Business Owners, Process Consultants** and many other roles are implemented simultaneously. These roles naturally have substantial overlaps regarding their skills, abilities and competencies. This is less risky if the relevant positions and persons can take on this role simultaneously. However, as soon as these roles are implemented independently by various stakeholders in the organisation, it becomes necessary to have highly experienced **Change** and **Conflict Managers** as full-time resources to manage the resulting friction.

The evolution of roles and professions

Automation will advance unstoppably with various technologies, such as artificial intelligence, and change professions and roles profoundly and permanently. This will have a significant impact on the world of work. Recognised professions will no longer have the same status. Jobs with repetitive and rule-based tasks will be automated, and employees will be expected to fulfil new requirements and skills not previously included in the training plan and degree curriculum. While this will create new jobs and professions, it will eliminate specific ones. Automation will mean that people working with repetitive and rule-based tasks must focus on more creative and complex aspects of their work. This, in turn, will lead to the emergence of new tasks that require skills such as problem-solving, critical and analytical thinking and emotional intelligence. Each and every individual will need to adapt and master new skills to remain relevant in the changing labour market. Lifelong learning and upskilling will be crucial as roles constantly evolve and change based on new skills. In turn, organisations must recognise and respond to these changes, identify new skills with foresight and develop their workforce at an early stage.

The potential of harmonised roles and processes

Roles and processes are frequently discussed together. This is because the combination of roles and processes regulates clear responsibilities and ensures an organisation's efficiency. Roles define the responsibilities and authorisations of individuals or groups, while processes describe the steps and workflows for completing specific tasks or achieving certain results. Linking roles and processes makes assigning tasks, tracking progress, and optimising workflows easier. Roles and processes are like a lock and key because they are interdependent. Without the key, the lock is  useless, and without the lock, the key cannot be used anywhere. They are directly interdependent and necessary to achieve the desired results and reach the goals.

Consideration of processes is also imperative when changing enterprise capabilities, organisational structures and roles, as processes provide the framework for how work is done in an organisation. When these changes occur, processes must constantly be reviewed and adapted to align with the new capabilities, structures and roles. Otherwise, this will lead to chaos and inefficiency, as unaligned processes will logically lead to confusion, miscommunication and lower productivity.

Although considering and combining roles and processes is a step in the right direction, it has unfortunately become too familiar for organisations to restrict their focus solely to modelling workflows with roles. Although these elements undoubtedly play an essential part in the wide world of process management, it is crucial to recognise that they are only part of the tip of the iceberg (see Figure 6). Challenge yourself to

6. **Beyond the surface: The holistic approach to an integrated (process) management system**

grow beyond the ordinary and adopt a mindset beyond these boundaries. The sheer power and potential in the depths of comprehensive process mapping go far beyond traditional process modelling as many know it. The enterprise capability of process management requires a holistic approach that encompasses the outer layers of process modelling and goes deep into the organisation's core. Imagine a world in which the intricacies of processes are perfectly synchronised with operational data and information, in which real-time data flows seamlessly through a networked system, in which automation and optimisation are finely interwoven and in which an organisation's various management systems are synchronised. This sounds too good to be true, but holistic process management makes it realistic and possible. To realise the full potential of process management, we need to open up, rethink traditional approaches to process management and embark on a transformative journey beyond simply modelling and documenting workflows with roles.

Processes as the backbone of your organisation

An essential part of an organisation is the multitude of daily activities that all employees carry out. These activities should be coordinated to achieve the desired results quickly, with high quality, and cost-effectively. We speak of business processes when considering all activities that produce a common business result. Business processes are performed and/or processed by people, systems, data, information, raw materials, or other resources to create business objects (outputs) and meet customer expectations and organisational goals.

Business processes are the backbone of any organisation, providing a structured framework for the workflow and guiding the entire operation through the complexity of an organisation. They define the flow of activities and the interplay of roles and responsibilities required to produce products and services. Similarly, data, systems, risks and many other variables are orchestrated along processes to fulfil the expectations of customers, shareholders and stakeholders. By clearly defining and structuring these processes, organisations ensure consistency, reliability, efficiency and effectiveness, promoting fluid workflows, better resource allocation and the ability to adapt quickly and flexibly to change. Ultimately, well-designed and executed business processes enable organisations to differentiate themselves from their competitors and ensure sustainable, innovative and healthy growth.

Business processes have different characteristics, so they are categorised into the following superordinate categories so that we can better distinguish between them.

- **Management processes** comprise a range of activities and measures that ensure an organisation's efficient and effective functioning. These processes focus on planning, organising, managing and controlling.

- **Core processes** are at the heart of an organisation. They contribute directly to the organisation's key objectives, vision, and mission. These business processes are essential for the organisation's operation, product or service provision, and achieving strategic goals.

- **Support processes** in an organisation are activities and measures that facilitate the smooth execution of the core processes and contribute to the organisation's overall functioning and effectiveness. In contrast to the core processes, which relate directly to the organisation's primary objectives, support processes provide essential support, resources, procedures, and infrastructure required for the efficient functioning of the core processes.

The necessity for process documentation and transparency

Let's look at these different business processes from a different angle. Would you undergo a surgical procedure without the surgeon having good medical expertise, appropriate medical equipment, surgical skills and specific knowledge of your disease and anatomy? Probably not, because the consequences can be catastrophic.

This is because all organs, bones, muscles, nerves, vessels, trace minerals and molecules (etc.) fulfil their purpose, work together like a symphony, and have complex interrelationships. The same applies to business processes. Business processes have equally diverse and complex interdependencies that are not always recognisable at first glance but are usually justified and necessary. Without these business processes, an organisation would collapse like a body without a skeleton. And just as the body cannot function without a skeleton, a skeleton cannot function without organs, bones, muscles, nerves, vessels, trace minerals and molecules (etc.). Similarly, a process requires people, machines, tools, vehicles, raw materials, and intangible resources such as energy and data to be executed and to transform defined requirements (inputs) into desired results (outputs).

Business processes have interdependencies that are not always recognisable at first glance, which is why we need to visualise them.

Many employees and BPM communities have been discussing and demanding process documentation for years. Yet, organisations are continuously 'transforming' and 'optimising' processes without creating and using this documentation or having a clear picture of their processes. There are hundreds of reasons for this, varying from organisation to organisation, industry to industry and culture to culture. Nevertheless, patterns originating in natural human behaviour, among other things, can be observed. It is so simple because what people do not see, hear, feel and sense is not transformed into knowledge through experience.

On the other hand, what I see, hear, feel, and sense is transformed into knowledge through experience, which can then be utilised elsewhere. In functional organisations, silos are promoted indirectly and usually unintentionally, which means that procedural and interdisciplinary connections are only transparent to a limited extent and are overlooked. The problem  here is not so much with the employees, as is often portrayed, but rather how collaboration between departments/silos is systematically promoted or prevented by organisational structures, process orientation and role definitions. But this is precisely why many projects and initiatives for process optimisation fail to deliver the expected results, and this limited view overlooks the true complexity of our organisations. Consequently, optimisation initiatives and projects become unforeseen wild journeys, as unexpected issues arise during the course of the journey that make it difficult to achieve the original goals, or budgets and timelines have to be redefined.

At the same time, many organisations and their structures have grown. As a result, employees have gradually lost the overview, and we have reached a state in which these structures and processes are no longer cognitively comprehensible, even if there is cross-divisional and procedural cooperation.

Another reason why process documentation is still not sufficiently used for process optimisation and reengineering is because the right way to document processes is still not understood. Many associate process documentation only with drawing flowcharts and are unaware of the impact that process transparency can have on the management of organisations. A flowchart with roles is undoubtedly a good start,

Many still associate process documentation ONLY with drawing flowcharts!

but how do I connect the process to other operational data and information essential to our transformative journey? Wouldn't it be a dream to see ad hoc which applications and systems support the process and whether they are interlinked with other applications and systems? Or wouldn't it be great if we could see which specific requirements from standards and laws have to be adhered to? And wouldn't it be brilliant to know which data or other objects (inputs/outputs), such as documents, instructions, materials, raw materials and more, are used or processed? It would also be excellent to know whether known risks accompany the process and whether necessary measures and controls have already been implemented or require attention (see Figure 7).

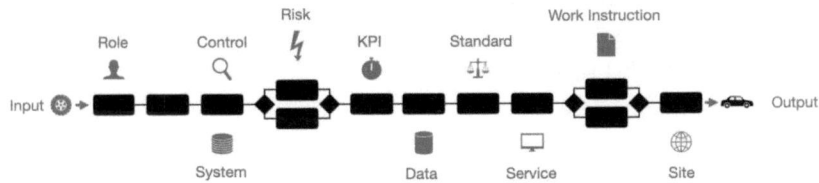

7.   **Operational data / information on the process model**

Here, we find ourselves in a vicious circle because we need transparency and the 'big picture' to create an awareness of the wealth of relationships and correlations. Still, we don't get this because there is no awareness of what is hidden behind a process. This brings us back to the topic of organisational structures because it is precisely these functional patterns of behaviour that make it essential to rethink the design of organisational structures.

These hidden or undocumented treasures will present an organisation with considerable challenges in an ever more rapidly and exponentially changing, increasingly digitalised and regulated world. After all, how can all these things be considered in the increasing transformation of processes? Similar to 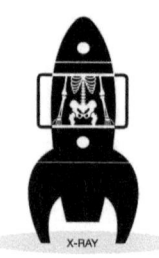 the example of surgery, we need an anamnesis of the patient with X-ray and MRI images as well as other 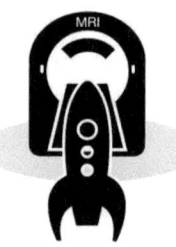 (imaging) procedures to diagnose requirements and necessary treatment paths preventively and to be able to react accordingly. Ultimately, every surgery should improve the patient's quality of life efficiently and effectively because none of us wants to undergo unnecessary and costly surgeries and must suffer a 'trial and error' method.

However, despite the known consequences, anamnesis must be performed more frequently in business processes. There is still a misconception that process mapping is too time-consuming and that employees know the processes inside out because they execute them daily. This supposedly saves time-consuming work, and new software systems and platforms already contain best practice processes, as many technology providers have successfully misleadingly propagated. However, even if they can provide support, relying purely on this technology is foolish. Otherwise, the tail will wag the dog, not vice versa.

In established structures and organisations, traditional and conventional measures often no longer work, and fundamental reorganisation measures are necessary to lead organisations into the new era. In addition, it is generally impossible to establish new processes on a green field. Therefore, providing a blueprint is crucial if you want to save investment and resources. It is, of course, true that process documentation can only be created with effort. However, it is also true that many optimisation and transformation projects suffer enormous time and cost losses because the complexity of organisations, systems, and processes is underestimated. **From this perspective, time and resources are there but must be used correctly and preventively.** Once transparency is in place, it will drive optimisation and transformation, accelerate them leanly and save enormous costs. This is not only because we then have beautifully visualised processes but also because process mapping unconsciously generates a tremendous asset in the minds of employees, which is then automatically available for optimisation and transformation projects. If technologies such as process mining and AI are used correctly, the time required to capture and generate all process information will hardly play a role, and the benefits will far outweigh the costs.

Technologies such as process mining and artificial intelligence will make process mapping more efficient.

Take away

Process mapping is not about creating great diagrams but about documenting complexity in a structured way so that we can answer multidimensional and complex questions with different views. If we succeed in synchronising people (e.g. employees), machines (e.g. BPM technology) and roles (e.g. process managers), the journey towards process excellence can begin.

Let's imagine the spaceship Enterprise again. Would we modify the propulsion system without safety precautions and construction plans if we knew it was directly connected to the life support system? Without a clear understanding of the intricate interactions and correlations, a mistake during repair could inadvertently disrupt the life support functions necessary for the crew's survival, and wouldn't that be too big a risk? Therefore, you should only start a repair with a detailed construction plan that contains additional information on people, materials, standards, etc.

Multiplying processes in a globalised world

Imagine you have a restaurant and detailed recipes with precisely defined steps for all your dishes. Now you want to expand into other countries and cook and serve your best dishes there. Would you then completely reinvent your recipe in that country? Or would you take your original recipe and only adapt some ingredients to the locally available ingredients or flavours? You probably wouldn't change the sequence of steps in your recipe either, as this would influence the result.

The early success story of McDonald's undeniably illustrates this in a remarkable and verifiable way. Richard and Maurice

McDonald perfected the burger preparation process. They played out the process on a tennis court with different arrangements of the kitchen equipment until it was almost perfect. With the 'Speedee System', it was possible to reduce customer interaction from order taking to food delivery to 30 seconds. **That was in 1948!** The system was then rolled out 1:1 and multiplied. As a result, Hamburgers and co. were and are still prepared efficiently, effectively, and reproducibly using precisely the same principles, whether in San Bernardino, New York, Paris, Tokyo, Munich or Rome.

Let's apply this approach to business processes because we can extend the discussion about the complexity of processes and the need to understand them thoroughly. International organisations with global supply chains have additional dimensions of complexity. One of these dimensions is the various locations the organisations have worldwide to achieve market proximity. As soon as such locations pursue the same business purpose and goals, business processes are 'multiplied'.

The more global and/or the more locations an organisation has, the greater and more important it is to utilise the resulting synergies. Ultimately, this is not just about the workflow and roles in processes but also about infrastructures and investments in projects, maintenance and consulting costs. In addition, different terminologies and nomenclatures are used for processes, activities, systems and/or business objects in such **If you have your processes under control, you can multiply them without exponentially increasing complexity and expenditure.** cases, which is not only due to language barriers and cultural differences. Process management with standards is also beneficial in connecting people along processes across languages, cultures, and continents. In other words, if you have your processes under control, you can multiply them without exponentially increasing complexity and expenditure.

BPM as the GPS for process transformation

'Process excellence' is a popular buzzword that is more of a target picture than a conceptual approach, as achieving process excellence requires a customised approach often referred to as business process management (BPM). BPM is critical to improvement and transformation as it provides a systematic approach to identifying, measuring, analysing, optimising, automating and controlling processes at both strategic and operational levels. This approach often uses technologies such as process modelling software, process intelligence and (workflow) automation tools to support process improvement initiatives. BPM aims to improve business performance by promoting collaboration, standardising processes, supporting agility and ensuring compliance. It provides a holistic view of an enterprise's process organisation to promote process quality and adaptability in a constantly evolving business environment.

To implement BPM, at least the following aspects must be taken into account:

- **Defined goals for excellent processes**: Measurable targets with defined metrics derived from the enterprise strategy.

- **Leadership and responsibility**: Assignment of roles and responsibilities and the target operating model description.

🔺 **Process documentation and analysis**: Creation of process transparency with standardised conventions and a process house with clear architectures and structures.

🔺 **Change management, communication and training**: Enabling the Process Excellence Community to work and act in a process-orientated manner and quickly train new employees in new processes.

🔺 **Process improvement and optimisation**: Continuous improvement of efficiency and effectiveness, supported by sufficient methods and tools.

🔺 **Technologies and systems**: Selection, definition and application of BPM software and tools.

🔺 **Definition of metrics/PPIs:** Definition of process performance indicators (PPI) to track progress at both operational and strategic levels.

🔺 **Advice and identification of improvement measures**: Encouraging feedback and actively developing suggestions for improvement.

🔺 **Control and monitoring**: Regular evaluation of objectives, measures and monitoring of governance.

The implementation and establishment of BPM requires a strategic approach with defined goals as well as role concepts with decision-making bodies, process models and architectures, methods and tools, metrics and measurement systems, as well as training, good change management and intensive involvement of stakeholders (see Figure 8). Furthermore, introducing BPM requires good planning of resources, milesto-

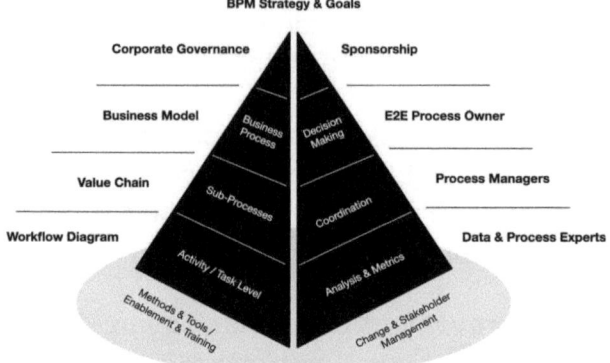

BPM Strategy & Goals

Corporate Governance — Sponsorship

Business Model — E2E Process Owner

Value Chain — Process Managers

Workflow Diagram — Data & Process Experts

Business Process / Decision Making / Sub-Processes / Coordination / Activity / Task Level / Analysis & Metrics / Methods & Tools / Enablement & Training / Change & Stakeholder Management

8. Business Process Management Pyramid

nes and funding, as well as resilience and patience, as the implementation requires far-reaching interventions in existing organisational structures. Support from top management is also crucial to promote willingness to change and to prevent BPM pioneers from being worn down by resistance from existing structures.

After all, the ultimate goal of BPM is to increase efficiency and effectiveness and thus improve the overall performance of the entire organisation. To achieve this, it is also essential to involve the relevant stakeholders from cross-functional areas such as IT, risk management, compliance, quality management, project management and strategy management in addition to the functional stakeholders.

The art of process improvement for customer loyalty and employee satisfaction

Managing an organisation without continuous process improvement is like managing a spaceship without regular maintenance and development. You will probably reach your destination, but inefficiencies and risks will hinder the journey. In many cases, continuous improvement is considered separately in organisations and carried out by operational excellence teams. However, it is an integral part of a holistic BPM concept and definitely does not only affect processes in operational business.

Regarding continuous improvement, organisations tend to focus exclusively on core processes to increase efficiency, optimise the use of resources, maintain quality standards and promote innovation. This is logical, as most resources are usually tied up in the core processes and, therefore, have the most significant leverage on operational efficiency. However, the overall support and management processes should be considered. Support processes are generally not carried out as frequently and, when considered separately, do not tie up as many, but usually costly, resources. Viewed as a whole, they also significantly influence costs, time, quality, efficiency, and effectiveness. Furthermore, these processes ensure the execution of the core processes by providing qualified employees and guaranteeing the framework conditions necessary to ensure the operation of the core processes in accordance with all internal and external requirements. Inefficient and ineffective support and management processes, therefore, inevitably lead to poor core processes.

Ultimately, all processes contribute to an overarching organisation's goal. Therefore, all processes have their justification and must be taken into account. This also means that all processes are interconnected in some way. You can think of it as a vast network with millions of correlations, and precisely, this complexity needs to be understood, mapped and visualised when it comes to process improvement. And if a process is not connected to the other processes in any way, then switch it off immediately!

If a process is not connected to the other processes, switch it off immediately!

But what constitutes process excellence, and how can we not only increase the efficiency and effectiveness of operational processes but also achieve an efficient and effective improvement and transformation process? This question is crucial, as large investments are made in improvement and transformation projects, which in many organisations take far too long and often do not deliver the desired results.

In addition to the need for more process management maturity and transparency, another reason why optimisation and transformation projects run inadequately can be found in the handling and application of the toolbox of project management and optimisation methods. There are some excellent methods, such as Lean Management, Six Sigma, Design Thinking, Agile and Hybrid Project Management, as well as Value Stream Mapping, PDCA, Kaizen, Requirement Engineering and many more, which have proven themselves in principle. Unfortunately, all these methods are often lumped together and not consistently implemented in many organisations. Many organisations are unaware of these methods and their potential or are confused about them. Even though some approaches and methods have commonalities and similarities, there are also significant differences. What all methods have in common, however, is that they not only require training and routine but also follow a fundamental attitude and philosophy. For example, Jack Welch at General Electric strongly promoted and established Six Sigma as a method. After he departed from General Electric, however, the use of Six Sigma initially declined sharply, as although it was rightly demanded top-down, it had apparently not become anchored in the organisation's culture at that time. It is, therefore, not enough to train individual employees in it, as roles and processes have to be implemented here, too, which must be manifested organisationally, and without them, the trained employees will only become lone warriors.

In addition, some of these methods are often criticised for being too time-consuming and complex to use. Admittedly, all methods require experience and routine in addition to training and education, but they are not complex methods in general; it is the processes that need to be handled and optimised with it, and the methods merely reveal this fact effectively. Conversely, this means that if we do not use these methods or only use them to a limited extent, we close our eyes and deny ourselves the true complexity of the processes, which then catches up with us during the optimisation and transformation projects.

It is also frequently observed that project managers are only temporary resources in organisations. Instead, employees from specialist departments are deployed and rotated from project to project as part-time project managers. Unfortunately, the resulting poor project outcomes are regularly attributed to the methods and discredited, even though the methods themselves are not the problem. As a result, tried and tested methods are regularly discarded, and new methods are proclaimed as the new holy grail and propagated worldwide. Moreover, organisations may be reluctant to deploy such resources as a full-time job because of budget constraints, competing priorities or lack of understanding of the return on investment. However, if you look honestly at the complexity of organisations, you will realise that such part-time roles need to become full-time jobs.

Another reason why project and optimisation methods are slow to gain acceptance can also be an overly hierarchical culture or rigid structures that are not conducive to the introduction of methods such as Six Sigma, Scrum or Lean Management, as these methods often promote flexibility, collaboration and personal responsibility, which can be at odds with traditional organisational structures. Ultimately, these methods are critical organisational capabilities that must be vigorously developed and require training, experience and routine, as well as solid support and encouragement from executive management. Furthermore, these methods must be integrated into support processes for continuous improvement and interlinked with other methods and stakeholders. This means that the individual methods do not contradict each other and should be combined. For large organisations, it makes sense to define their own Business Process Improvement Process (BPIP), which becomes the standard, covers individual needs and combines the best of the various methods. Such a process also brings together different stakeholders and considers enterprise-specific and binding requirements that must be considered when optimising and redesigning processes.

In the past, many process optimisations and transformations were also tackled using traditional and selected optimisation or project management methods, which worked to a certain extent. However, due to increasing internal and external requirements, project managers must consider many new complex issues to ensure business process conformity. Data, interfaces, applications, standards, regulations, responsibilities and much more are affected or changed during process optimisation and transformation. At the same time, the requirements for information security, compliance, quality management, risk management and IT management must be met. The individual coordination of all these requirements and stakeholders is a risky business, and traditional project management approaches are geared towards something other than this. A business process improvement process tailored to the organisation's needs, helps project managers to consider the key requirements to make the optimisation and/or transformation process as efficient and effective as possible while staying on time and within budget.

Incidentally, many of the abovementioned requirements must be considered when improving and redesigning processes arising from an organisation's various management systems.

Maximising efficiency with an IMS

The combination of several management systems within a standardised framework is called an integrated management system (IMS). Organisations use an IMS as a structure to effectively plan, coordinate and control their internal and external requirements. It comprises strategies, processes, procedures and practices that control decision-making, the allocation of responsibilities and performance measurement in various functional areas of an organisation. An IMS, therefore, combines multiple disciplines and processes such as strategy management, quality management, environmental management, health and safety management, compliance and risk management, as well as enterprise architecture management and information security management.

An IMS aims to streamline and harmonise these different management systems to enable easier coordination, communication and synergy between them. By integrating the various management disciplines, organisations can avoid duplication of effort, reduce risk, minimise conflict and improve overall efficiency and effectiveness.

BPM is an excellent connector and foundation for an IMS, as most of the information other stakeholders and management systems are interested in is created, managed and controlled along processes. Thus, parallel management systems can consume the documented processes and responsibilities and bring their information, such as data categories, compliance and risk monitoring requirements, IT infrastructure, quality standards, regulatory requirements, projects and strategic objectives, etc., into the BPM system. Moreover, this data can be linked across the management systems, allowing organisations to gain additional information in the context of the associated processes and implement the necessary measures and actions.

In the future, it will become increasingly important for those responsible for the various management systems to integrate and work together. This is due to the growing risks in the supply chain, increasing regulations, digitalisation, globalisation, and legal and third-party requirements. As a result, organisations face even more complexity and need professional management to overcome these challenges. This also includes a corresponding process, as described in the previous chapter, which ensures that all requirements are considered and complied with when changes are made.

However, integrating management systems is also essential from the perspective of the specialist departments because, let's imagine that all of the stakeholders above in an organisation contact the departments independently of each other. For example, project management and those responsible for risk management and information security could simultaneously request information about systems and data as well as risks and controls from the same target groups. This would lead to time-consuming and resource-intensive duplication of work, and the organisation would also have to deal with different terminology and nomenclature. As a result, an uncoordinated approach of varying management systems would complicate the organisation and thus limit efficiency, effectiveness and productivity, as well as massively increase costs and risks.

Take Away

The increasing dependence on technology and digital tools will lead to new cooperation models. Organisations will only be successful if they form cross-functional teams that take responsibility and make decisions based on defined competencies and roles. This is inevitably necessary to adapt quickly and flexibly to new environmental conditions. Organisations need to break down silos by reorganising enterprise capabilities, organisational structures and responsibilities (roles) and empowering employees to understand their business processes and make decisions faster to keep up with the pace of 'digital' transformation. Well-defined and documented business processes play a crucial role. They are the foundation for optimisation and transformation to ensure smooth processes and achieve the desired results in the long term. A holistic process for improving business processes, in turn, ensures that the requirements of a wide range of stakeholders are systematically taken into account and that the optimisation and transformation of processes are streamlined. Ultimately, the unfolding power of processes also lies in bringing together and connecting as many players as possible who are responsible for the various management systems in an integrated management system.

Business process management system[4] (BPMS) vs. quality management system (QMS)

Quality management systems (QMS) and business process management systems (BPMS) are often compared and confused, but let's get one thing straight: They are **NOT** the same! While commonalities, overlaps and similarities exist, they are fundamentally different management systems. QMS ensures the quality of products and services, compliance with standards and laws, and customer satisfaction. It is about perfecting the end result. In contrast, a BPMS is about optimising the entire process and involving other stakeholders.

While both systems aim to improve processes and increase success, the QMS is narrower in scope and focuses primarily on product and service quality and the processes affected by them. At the same time, a BPMS takes a more comprehensive approach to managing all aspects of the processes. So, let's stop mixing them up and appreciate the unique value of both systems!

A business process management system (BPMS) is a holistic approach to managing and optimising the organisation's end-to-end processes. It involves coordinating people, processes,

---

[4] Definition: A system is a set of interconnected and interdependent components or parts that work together to achieve a common goal or purpose. Systems can be physical or conceptual and exist within larger systems. System and software are often used interchangeably, but they are not.

policies and technologies to achieve operational efficiency, agility and strategic goals. The software-independent interpretation of a BPMS covers the entire lifecycle of a business process, from design and implementation to monitoring, analysis and continuous improvement. It is about establishing a culture of process-oriented thinking in the organisation, promoting collaboration and ensuring the alignment of processes with the overall business strategy. This broader perspective emphasises the organisational mindset and the methods used to improve processes and systematically achieve sustainable business excellence.

In contrast, the quality management system specialises in managing and maintaining the quality of products and services and the relevant processes within an organisation (even if some disagree). To this end, quality standards must be defined, and quality processes must be controlled and ensured so that products and services fulfil or exceed predefined quality criteria. The QMS, therefore, primarily comprises functions for defining quality standards, tracking corresponding measurements, conducting audits, managing corrective and preventive actions (CAPA) and maintaining quality documentation. The QMS primarily involves quality control teams, quality managers, quality inspectors, and auditors who are responsible for compliance with quality standards and legal requirements.

Both the business process management system (BPMS) and the quality management system (QMS) require documentation, measurement of processes, and continuous improvement. While a BPMS focuses on increasing the efficiency and effectiveness of business processes, a QMS focuses explicitly on quality standards and control. Close cooperation is required as the two systems cannot be completely separate due to the individual design of each system.

To summarise, business process management systems (BPMS) and quality management systems (QMS) pursue superficially similar objectives. Both systems also use very similar or identical terminology, but the underlying definitions are quite different. A BPMS aims to optimise business processes to improve efficiency and effectiveness, considering all process-related dimensions. At the same time, a QMS specialises in maintaining and continuously improving the quality of products and services by complying with standards, regulations, and any other internally defined requirements. Even though the two systems are different approaches, they should be closely linked in order to utilise their overlaps.

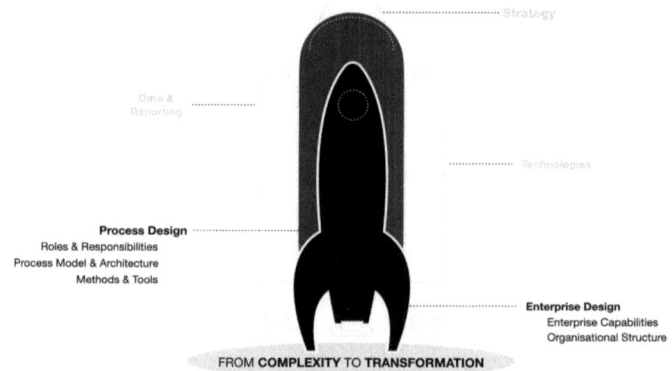

9. Process Excellence Enterprise: From roles to smart processes

'It's not the strongest species that survives, nor the most intelligent. It is the one that can best adapt to change.'

- Charles Darwin -

4. From technologies to valuable platforms

Think again of your organisation as a spaceship and the different technologies as the components needed for a successful launch and exploration. Just as a spaceship needs a combination of propulsion, navigation, communication, life support systems and a well-trained crew with sophisticated skills to reach its destination safely, your business processes also benefit from the interplay of multiple technologies and well-trained employees.

Using only one technology for the spaceship or business process management would be like trying to launch a rocket with only one engine but no guidance system, communication with ground control or life support systems for the crew. It might temporarily boost you, but you wouldn't get anywhere.

Combining the various benefits of BPM technologies is crucial as it enables a comprehensive and synergistic approach to improving and reorganising business processes. The isolated use of a BPM tool or technology without a holistic BPM approach can also bring some short-term improvements in managing business processes. However, you will never be able to maximise its full potential in this way, and there is a risk that processes will become increasingly complex and complicated over time in the overall context of an organisation. Especially if different responsibilities manage and functionally utilise these BPM technologies. Many BPM technologies have their purpose and justification but only fulfil functionalities that need to be systematically integrated into the organisation's ecosystem and orchestrated with each other in a process-oriented manner (e.g. as part of a business process improvement process). It is, therefore, alarming that such BPM technologies and tools are still operated in parallel and uncoordinated by different departments and functions in many organisations. The business process management approach is actually decades ahead of its time and calls for a holistic approach. For the analysis, optimisation, automation, transformation and monitoring of business processes, it is therefore essential and crucial to define and coordinate the use and combination of BPM technologies along the entire lifecycle of business processes. Furthermore, as some of these BPM technologies have overlapping and redundant capabilities and functions, a central accountability is necessary to oversee their utilisation and co-ordination.

Utilising the synergy of multiple BPM technologies is crucial to taking your business to new heights. Different technologies can be used and combined. For example, business process management software (BPM software) is a comprehensive solution for mapping, monitoring and optimising business processes. It is a powerful tool that can also be combined with various management methods such as strategy management, metric management, risk management, learning management and quality management. Process mining and intelligence is a data-driven technology that uses algorithms and techniques to analyse event logs from various software systems to visualise and analyse process data in real-time in order to optimise business processes. Another technology is Robotic Process Automation (RPA), which is used for process automation to automate repetitive and rule-based tasks and reclaim human labour for value-adding tasks. Workflow management technology ensures that tasks are completed on time by coordinating successive tasks and assigning them to the right people (roles). Then there is artificial intelligence (AI) and machine learning (ML), which are used for predictive analytics, natural language processing, anomaly detection and automation. The Internet of Things (IoT), in turn, is a network of physical devices, vehicles, appliances and other objects equipped with sensors, software and connectivity so that they can connect with each other and exchange data. Collaboration software is also included in this technology mix to facilitate and promote communication and collaboration between team members. Finally, there is digital twin technology, a virtual and digital representation of a physical object, system or process with real-time data and simulation models to perform analyses, simulations, optimisations and monitoring.

In general, it's a beautiful flower bouquet of powerful tools that help organisations streamline their operations, understand complexity faster and better, reduce costs and increase efficiency. However, they will not release their full potential if they are used independently and separately from each other. So, let's take a closer look at some of these technologies to better understand their purpose.

Unlocking synergies with software for BPM

Business process management software provides a systematic approach to managing, designing, modelling, executing, monitoring and analysing processes. It forms the basis and should be the starting point for any BPM or process excellence initiative.

Business processes are complex networks, and depending on the perspective, they can be defined horizontally, vertically, or diagonally. In general, it is not possible to determine a definitive 'right' or 'wrong' position in this context; instead, there is a degree of confusion when different perspectives are applied to a particular process. BPM software is, therefore, primarily used to map an organisation's process model and the underlying architecture from a common perspective. It is the leading system in business process management and the basis for all other systems that benefit from these process structures.

As soon as the process model and architecture have been created and the business model has been mapped in terms of processes, a core functionality is the modelling and design of the processes. Although this is initially a time investment, it forms the basis for sustainable process management and integration with other management systems.

Of course, a process model with modelled flowcharts is still of limited value. Still, suppose the processes are now supplemented and linked with valuable operational information such as systems, data, risks, standards, requirements, training, responsibilities, projects, strategies, goals, metrics, etc. In that case, there are a considerable number of use cases for operationalising these process models.

This makes it possible to align an organisation's business processes with its strategy and goals to prioritise the right processes. It is also possible to visualise and analyse the information architecture of processes to derive strategic harmonisation and standardisation potential. BPM software also promotes a culture of continuous improvement by encouraging the analysis of processes and looking for ways to reveal and understand complex interrelationships and inefficiencies. BPM software also helps to ensure compliance with regulations and internal guidelines by formulating process requirements and providing audit trails. In addition, BPM software often includes collaboration features that promote communication and teamwork between employees involved in the processes, contributing to a cross-functional corporate culture.

A roadmap for the successful implementation of BPM software

Implementing BPM software requires a strategic and conceptual approach to ensure seamless integration into an organisation's processes. The various BPM software solutions on the market differ in detail, and all have advantages and disadvantages. When choosing a BPM software solution, you must define your requirements and objectives to select the right solution. Factors such as scalability, flexibility and user-friendliness are standard requirements that BPM software should fulfil. Another requirement is to ensure seamless integration with existing or future BPM tools, such as process mining, or other management systems, such as quality management systems.

However, a clear picture of the process architecture must be developed and derived from the business model before business processes are created and modelled in the BPM software. Various process reference models can be used for this purpose. Another aspect is the definition and interpretation of a notation (usually BPMN2.0), which must be defined according to the individual requirements and ideally as simply as possible.

In addition to the process architecture and notation, it is then necessary to determine what information (e.g. about systems, data, roles, regulations, etc.) must be included in the modelling. There is also no right or wrong here, and each organisation must determine this for itself based on its specific requirements. However, the more information is made available in a standardised format (from defined libraries), the more beneficial the documentation will be for the various stakeholders. Or, in other words the less structured information is provided, the less you will benefit from BPM software.

An authorisation and role concept must also be created to ensure that defined information and processes can only be changed and released by authorised employees. Transparency wins when it comes to reading rights, which is why reading rights should not be restricted.

As soon as the technical basis is established, a process model with a defined architecture, process conventions, interfaces and libraries, and an authorisation and role concept are set up and implemented; appropriate target group-specific training courses still need to be developed.

Drawing up an implementation plan now makes sense, depending on the organisation's size. Here, it is advantageous if a business process management approach is linked to an organisation's overall strategy to derive the most critical processes. In addition, organisational aspects such as core areas, locations, risks, and the connection to other management systems must be considered.

Ultimately, introducing a measurement system for process maturity is an elementary tool that should be introduced with every BPM software implementation, as this allows tracking the progress and quality of the established processes and, as a result, the BPM software to be continuously monitored. It is essential to keep such models pragmatic and not approach them too scientifically because if such models are set up too extensively, they cannot be realised in practice. It is better to start with the first prioritised aspects and develop the process maturity model further as the process maturity develops.

Take Away

BPM software for business process management is like a conductor in a symphony, bringing all your processes together in perfect harmony. But it is more than just a central hub for managing processes. It also opens the door to an integrated management system. An integrated management system enables you to eliminate inefficiencies all at once, streamlining your processes and boosting overall effectiveness. No more isolated information and duplication of work! Instead, you get a streamlined and interconnected ecosystem where processes and data flow seamlessly. However, additional systems and tools are available and necessary to unleash the full power of the BPM framework. These systems, such as process mining, data analytics, robotic process automation and artificial intelligence, need to work closely with the BPM software to enhance its capabilities and extend its reach. Together, they form a powerful arsenal that maximises the benefits of BPM.

Many organisations have been using BPM software for a long time and have invested much time and effort in documenting processes in recent years. Nevertheless, a considerable proportion of them have done so in the absence of structured libraries and/or an explicit process model with clearly defined architectures. This is where it gets complicated because there will probably be no other option than to start from scratch.

The spaceship Enterprise now runs on a powerful new engine called business process management software. With their BPM software and Freddy's 1.9 turbo hamster wheel drive, the crew was now speeding through the universe. Freddy was so excited by the speed that he could hardly calm down, but slowly and steadily, he became utterly exhausted. The BPM software had increased the Enterprise's speed to the maximum, and poor Freddy could no longer keep up. He was stumbling around, which amused the rest of the crew. What they didn't realise was that the fault wasn't Freddy's. It was the lack of compatibility between the BPM software and the other systems (e.g. the old 1.9 turbo hamster wheel drive). The interactions of this powerful engine had not been considered, resulting in Freddy's comedic running style. After the crew burst into tears of joy, they realised they needed to rethink their approach. The BPM software was powerful but must be better aligned with the entire spaceship. On the one hand, Freddy and the hamster wheel were overloaded entirely, but on the other hand, the BPM software was still underpowered.

Discover treasures with process mining

One of the other technologies mentioned at the beginning is process mining. Process mining is a powerful, innovative technology that enables deep insights into business processes. It uncovers valuable data and insights that have been 'swallowed up' by IT systems during digitisation and have remained hidden for a long time. This will become more prevalent as organisations increasingly rely on IT systems to execute their processes. Process-related data is, therefore, the new oil of process design, and technologies, such as process mining, are the refineries that transform this data into valuable information.

Process mining unearths hidden data treasures by analysing event logs in IT systems, reconstructing the underlying processes, and contextually bringing them to the surface. Thus, process mining reconstructs the actual execution of processes and provides objective information on process performance. In this way, organisations can identify inefficiencies, deviations, and compliance problems and analyse them at unprecedented speed.

The beauty of process mining is that it bridges the gap between the digital and physical (manual) aspects of process execution. With process mining, organisations can utilise the power of their data even more efficiently and effectively and gain a comprehensive understanding of how their processes

One thing is already clear: the process world is full of treasures.

work in reality. With these valuable insights, organisations can make fast, data-driven decisions, increase efficiency, gain a competitive advantage in today's digitalised business landscape, and achieve significant cost savings.

Monitoring process performance: functional vs end-to-end

Let's first take a look at how process mining can be used. The first question is always which process to start with. To select the proper process, it is necessary to determine what is to be achieved with process mining and how this technology can contribute to fulfilling the organisation's objectives. Classic use cases include increasing efficiency and effectiveness, reducing operating costs, increasing automation and digitalisation and/or better control of process risks (compliance).

Once the objectives and processes have been defined, the data sources are evaluated, and the data is collected and extracted from the source systems. The collected data is then subjected to pre-processing, which includes cleansing, transformation, and structuring. Here, it is essential to examine the

BPM software to ensure that the process structures created are identical and fit together. The final step is the validation and conformity check.

Now, it's time to get started. But where to start? As soon as you move up the sliders in the process visualisation, you will see an incredible spaghetti diagram with millions of connections and thousands of activities. One thing is now clear: the process world is full of opportunities. You now have the ability to measure process performance end-to-end. So please resist the temptation to jump straight into optimisations and use cases without building real end-to-end structures, analytics and dashboards.

Let us assume that implementation is primarily aimed at increasing efficiency and effectiveness; you have evaluated a defined business process and a use case for automating an activity in the process. You now implement the automation, measure the automation rate of this activity, and quickly reach 80 per cent. That sounds fantastic and like an initial success, but what does this mean for the customer or the continuous increase in efficiency and effectiveness along the end-to-end process? The automation rate of 80 per cent may be meaningless because it says **nothing** about the impact on the end-to-end process. For example, it may be a consistent improvement in productivity and/or lead time of over 60 per cent or more, but it may only be 2 per cent or less. Without a true end-to-end view, it is impossible to recognise what has triggered automation along the end-to-end process (see Figure 10). This can also mean that the automation was functionally successful but, at the same time, may have led to a bottleneck in the subsequent flow of the process, as subsequent process participants can no longer keep up. In the worst-case scenario, automation would not have been necessary because an upstream improvement would have eliminated the automated activity entirely. Thus, automation is not an end in itself, and every process optimisation must be aligned with the objectives of an end-to-end business process. This does not necessarily mean that automation, as described here as an example, cannot still be helpful. Nevertheless, other use cases that remain undetected without an end-to-end view could be much more influential and/or process-related correlations could be overlooked.

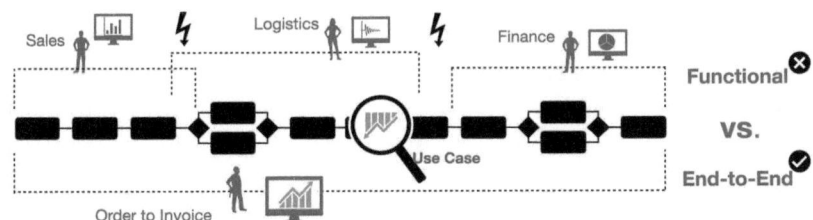

10. End-to-end vs. functional process analysis / measurement

Of course, you can still start with a small use case (low-hanging fruits) and learn. However, it remains essential to define end-to-end process structures, targets and process performance indicators (PPIs) and to measure the end-to-end as-is values and determine the end-to-end target values, as this is the only way to determine the actual impact of the use cases on the end-to-end business process and thus on efficiency and effectiveness. A pure use case-related optimisation without end-to-end process structures also bears the risk of further complicating processes without immediately noticing this.

Unfortunately, process mining implementations are often use case driven and too often detached from a business process management approach. This is usually done to demonstrate the ROI (return on investment) for the associated investments as quickly as possible. With this approach, however, the true value, which is usually far greater, cannot be demonstrated. Therefore, implementing process mining technology should be strongly recommended and combined with a business process management approach for the efficient and sustainable management of processes and complexity.

Once you have connected several end-to-end business processes and determined their as-is values and defined target values, you can also aggregate your process performance indicators so that you can monitor and report on the development of your process optimisation projects and transformation initiatives, as well as the associated investments at the top level. Once again, however, this is only possible if you have established and implemented genuine end-to-end process structures.

How process mining works together with BPM software

Be aware that process mining is fundamentally and conceptually an integral part of business process management (BPM) as it fulfils various and essential aspects of a BPM approach. With process mining, measuring the performance of processes has never been easier. Data-based process analyses are now standardised, super-fast and, for the first time, actually process- and **not** function-oriented. Using data-driven insights from event data in IT systems facilitates process analyses and delivers well-founded decisions for sustainable process improvements. Process mining also plays a vital role in regulatory compliance and internal audits, enabling organisations to track and ensure compliance based on data.

Combined with BPM software, both systems have large amounts of complementary data and information that they can exchange to gain a holistic view of processes and make it even easier for users to understand and utilise this information in a process-related context.

For example, it is possible to visualise process performance data and transactional information in BPM software at different levels (e.g. business process, sub-process, activity) along the defined process architectures. It is now also easier to identify manual activities for digitalisation and to evaluate the conformity or deviation between defined and executed processes. Furthermore, the BPM software can utilise information such as risks, controls, responsibilities, projects, the organisation's goals, metrics, and much more operational information. This makes it possible to identify and organise further potential along the digitally reconstructed and visualised processes, which is not necessarily related to efficiency and effectiveness but is not less critical for organisations. However, this method of collaborating with software programmes is still in its infancy, and several exciting use cases will arise from this connection over the next few years.

Take Away

Process mining is an integral part of BPM as it provides advanced process insights and data-driven analysis required to understand, monitor, optimise and continuously improve business processes. On the other hand, BPM software provides further information about manual process activities, responsibilities, information architecture and other stakeholders' requirements (e.g. compliance, risk management, quality management, etc.) that are equally essential for collaborative and sustainable process design. It helps BPM professionals make informed decisions and take actions to increase operational efficiency by considering all aspects and aligning processes with business objectives.

Process mining is one of the missing pieces of the BPM puzzle when it comes to organising processes holistically. In textbooks and BPM theory, process analysis and monitoring have been described and demanded as important BPM factors for decades but have hardly been possible. In practice, process analysis and continuous monitoring with traditional tools have proven to be very time-consuming and laborious. So, let's combine process mining and BPM software to ensure a sustainable increase in process performance.

Beyond mining: process intelligence is changing the game

Process intelligence is the BPM champions league and an add-on that goes beyond traditional process mining by providing advanced real-time analytics and predictive capabilities to gain an even deeper understanding of an organisation's business processes.

Process mining usually focuses on visualising process flows and extracting data from event logs to retrospectively identify bottlenecks and/or inefficiencies. Process intelligence, on the other hand, utilises real-time data to gain dynamic and up-to-date insights into process performance.

Imagine a manufacturing organisation that wants to optimise its production line. Process mining can help visualise the steps involved in the production process and highlight potential areas for improvement based on historical data. However, process intelligence goes one step further and analyses real-time data from sensors and machines (e.g. on the production line). This enables deviations from the normal process flow to be recognised at an early stage, system failures to be predicted, and predictive recommendations to be made to avoid costly downtime. Another example is customer service. Process mining can provide information on how customer enquiries are processed and identify common problems. On the other hand, process intelligence can analyse data in real-time to identify patterns of customer dissatisfaction, predict customer needs and recommend personalised solutions to improve customer satisfaction.

Process intelligence is a sophisticated technology that involves continuous real-time monitoring of ongoing processes and provides up-to-the-minute transparency. By incorporating advanced analytical techniques, process intelligence uncovers hidden insights in the process data, such as trends, patterns and anomalies that are not recognisable through traditional process mining. Process intelligence also includes predictive analytics to forecast future performance, potential bottlenecks and problems. Even prescriptive recommendations can be made based on predictive analyses and best practices. Imagine combining BPM software with process mining and process mining with process intelligence capabilities. This is a dream come true for all business process management enthusiasts because these technologies allow us to turn 'process excellence' into a reality.

Imagine if we combined BPM software with process mining and process mining with process intelligence capabilities. A dream would come true.

Competition of the intelligences: BI vs. PI

The competition between business intelligence (BI)[5] and process intelligence (PI) has gradually intensified in some enterprises. Both concepts offer valuable insights, but the question remains: Which intelligence will dominate or be used for what?

Business intelligence is the established player with which large amounts of data can be collected, analysed and interpreted to make informed decisions. The focus is on providing historical and real-time information about various aspects of a business, such as sales, profit, costs, customer behaviour and market trends. With BI, enterprises can recognise patterns, identify opportunities and make strategic decisions to improve the business's overall performance.

A more comprehensive and strategic approach is to integrate both intelligences.

On the other hand, process intelligence has proven to be an increasingly promising candidate. Process intelligence looks at an organisation's operational aspects in detail and reconstructs workflows to identify and eliminate inefficiencies through root cause analyses and process correlations.

Strictly speaking, however, there is no stringent separation between the two opponents, and there are shades of grey between black (BI) and white (PI). Moreover, both concepts

---

[5] 'Collective term for the IT-supported access to information, as well as the IT-supported analysis and processing of this information.' https://wirtschaftslexikon.gabler.de/definition/business-intelligence-29438/version-253044
Revision of Business Intelligence [as at 19/02/2018]

have their advantages and are not mutually exclusive. A more comprehensive and conceptual approach is integrating both intelligences to capitalise on their strengths. By combining the data-driven insights of BI with the process-oriented and structured analysis of PI, the information gained becomes more valuable than ever. The risk here is not so much the use of both concepts but instead that they provide different information when used independently, leading to friction and wrong decisions.

Business intelligence and process intelligence must be understood as complementary forces, and it must be defined as what is to be achieved with which concepts and tools, where which information is to be processed and visualised, and in what form. This must be defined individually and set out in a corresponding governance. By using both intelligences, organisations can exploit the potential of data-driven insights and process optimisation. As with so many things, both players must agree on a common denominator: the data basis and data quality. Nothing is more dangerous than receiving metrics and information from two systems that ultimately lead to different interpretations and decisions. By integrating the strengths of both intelligences, BI data can be contextualised using process information and thus consumed more comprehensibly. In contrast, PI can benefit from structured material, customer and supplier master data, and transactional information to perform **360° process analyses**.

In summary, the competition between business intelligence and process intelligence does not necessarily have to be a winner-takes-all scenario. By integrating the strengths of **business intelligence** and **process intelligence,** organisations can maximise their **human** intelligence to lead their business into an era where data-driven decisions enable the leap to pole position.

Increase added value with RPA bots

Another technology already mentioned is robotic process automation (RPA). RPA is a technology that automates repetitive and rule-based tasks typically performed by humans. RPA software uses so-called software robots or 'bots' to mimic human interactions with digital systems by capturing and manipulating data, triggering responses and executing actions. These bots can work across different applications, systems and databases to perform tasks that enable interaction with multiple software platforms. RPA bots can also be programmed to closely follow legal regulations and policies, reducing non-compliance risk. With rapid implementation and easy integration into existing systems and applications, RPA enables organisations to realise benefits and optimise end-to-end processes and data transfer quickly.

RPA can automate processes, reduce errors and relieve human labour.

RPA has gained popularity as such bots are easy to implement and can quickly streamline operations, reduce errors and reclaim human labour to focus on higher value-added tasks. They can process large amounts of data and complete tasks around the clock, increasing efficiency and productivity. RPA bots are most effective in processes with standardised and structured data. RPA bots may need to be supplemented by other technologies (such as artificial intelligence) or manual intervention for more complex processes or tasks that require cognitive decision-making.

As promising as this sounds, RPA also has limitations and challenges that organisations should be aware of. RPA bots lack cognitive abilities such as understanding natural language, context or emotions. They can perform tasks based on predefined rules (unattended), which makes them unsuitable for tasks that require decision-making, creativity or complex problem-solving. In addition, they may need assistance (attended) with processes that involve frequent changes or unstructured data, as they rely on predefined logic and structured input.

Although RPA can lead to long-term cost savings, there are investments and costs associated with the selection, implementation and maintenance of RPA tools. These include the costs of licensing, development, maintenance and training. In some cases, RPA needs to interact with legacy systems and applications, which can be challenging due to a lack of standardised interfaces and the need for customised integrations. The integration of RPA into existing IT infrastructures and applications can be complex, especially in large organisations with heterogeneous IT architectures and technologies. It is also worth noting that RPA bots need to be regularly monitored, maintained and updated to function effectively.

As always, there are two sides to the coin because even if implementing an RPA solution is supposedly easy, it can quickly become a business risk if organisations do not have the necessary skills and do not take precautions. It is essential to understand that RPA is not a one-size-fits-all solution for every process, no matter how temptingly easy it is to implement. Organisations must create specific responsibilities, roles, processes and rules for RPA bots to prevent chaotic and uncontrolled implementation. This includes a thorough assessment and analysis of processes to determine whether they need to be automated or would benefit more from optimisation or reengineering. Implementing RPA without a complete

Implementing RPA without understanding the process only leads to poor manual processes being converted into poor RPA processes.

understanding of the underlying processes will result in poor manual processes being converted into poor RPA processes, exacerbating inefficiencies rather than improving them.

Furthermore, the maintenance of RPA bots is a critical factor that is often overlooked. Software updates and releases of the systems in which these bots operate need to be closely monitored and accounted for. Otherwise, this will result in bots not functioning correctly and disrupting workflows. This emphasises the need for dedicated resources, responsibilities, skills and processes to ensure the proper maintenance and support of RPA

bots throughout their lifecycle. Similarly, this technology must be considered in conjunction with BPM software and process mining, as these technologies can be used to identify and assess the suitable RPA use cases and realise their actual value together.

Take Away

The biggest challenge in implementing RPA is that these tools are advertised as easy to implement. In reality, however, they are not plug-and-play solutions, as without a process-related context, more risks than benefits can arise. A good understanding of processes and the organisational need for new skills, responsibilities, resources and roles, as well as processes and guidelines, are mandatory for a successful RPA implementation. Of course, it is also advisable to consider an RPA implementation in the context of other BPM methods and technologies (e.g., BPM software or process mining) and integrate these into the entire process lifecycle.

Furthermore, finding the right balance between process optimisation and RPA automation is relevant. It is not always necessary to fully optimise a process before implementing an RPA bot. This is especially true at a time when IT is a perpetual bottleneck, and the rapid benefits of automation are clear and significant. Therefore, it is necessary to assess each situation individually and consider the potential benefits of in-depth process optimisation and short-term RPA automation. In general, the introduction of RPA can be a further catalyst for process improvements in the direction of process excellence if it is implemented professionally and responsibly in terms of organisation and processes and is driven by conscious decisions.

BPMS - RPA partnership: Triumphant synergy

The potential owners and 'administrators' of RPA solutions are very different within organisations. However, for the reasons mentioned above, it is highly advisable to place RPA solutions in the hands of BPM-oriented departments or communities (e.g. centres of process excellence). BPM-oriented departments and communities are responsible for monitoring and optimising business processes

RPA is not a one-size-fits-all solution.

throughout the organisation in close coordination with the specialist departments (e.g. process owners and subject matter experts). They deeply understand end-to-end processes, including their complexity and weaknesses. With this knowledge, they can identify the areas where RPA solutions can have the most significant impact. By taking organisational responsibility for RPA solutions, BPM-focused departments can ensure that automation efforts are aligned with the organisation's overall strategy and goals and that the right processes are selected for automation.

They can also coordinate the efforts of the various departments and stakeholders involved in the RPA implementation, ensuring a collaborative and coherent approach and mitigating the abovementioned risks. Furthermore, BPM experts can orchestrate the interaction with other BPM tools to ensure holistic and sustainable process improvements and efficient integration and utilisation of BPM technologies.

However, besides BPM experts, other stakeholders need to be involved in managing RPA solutions. One of these stakeholders is the IT, the technological infrastructure's guardian. The IT department also has the technical expertise to orchestrate the integration of the RPA software into the existing IT infrastructure and thus ensure smooth communication and data exchange. Furthermore, the IT department can provide the necessary support for troubleshooting technical problems that may arise during the operation of RPA bots.

Artificial intelligence revolutionises BPM

Artificial intelligence (AI) epitomises human ingenuity and is the pinnacle of current technological advancements. It is an extraordinary branch of computer science that enables machines to learn to 'think' and perform complex tasks that usually require human intelligence. At its core, AI harnesses the power of sophisticated algorithms and data processing capabilities to analyse vast amounts of information, recognise patterns and make or provide informed decisions. With the advancement of AI, we are on the cusp of a new era in which machine intelligence significantly complements and strengthens human capabilities.

AI technologies offer significant advantages in various business process management (BPM) scenarios. One of these scenarios is the ability to increase the efficiency of pure process modelling. With the help of AI, the creation of process flows and process models can be accelerated by creating or suggesting a process model instead of starting on a blank 'sheet'. AI can also generate text suggestions for business and sub-processes as well as activity descriptions, eliminating the need for time-consuming process descriptions. Another practical application of AI is process optimisation, where large data sets are analysed to identify bottlenecks, inefficiencies, deviations and areas for improvement. By providing such insights, AI enables organisations to optimise workflows, simplify fraud detection, improve resource allocation and thus increase the overall performance of processes.

Another exciting application is predictive analytics, where AI uses historical data to predict future trends, enabling companies to make proactive decisions and strategic plans. AI technologies contribute to decision support by providing information and recommendations in real time. Chatbots and virtual assistants driven by AI are increasingly crucial in interacting with customers, answering enquiries, and speeding up routine tasks. In addition, AI can create reports by automatically analysing large amounts of data and providing insights.

The most familiar scenario of AI integration is the automation of routine and rule-based tasks. AI can streamline processes by taking over data entry, document classification and simple decision-making, increasing operational efficiency and allowing employees to focus on more complex and value-adding activities.

AI can seamlessly be integrated into BPM to achieve greater agility, data-driven insights, and operational efficiency. However, the integration of AI also comes with several hurdles and limitations, and blind faith in this promising technology also harbours enormous risks. These risks include data quality, mitigating biases, building trust and change management. Furthermore, we should not  completely outsource our common sense, contextual understanding and creative thinking to AI. By implementing ethical guidelines, promoting transparency and explainability, and incorporating human expertise, organisations can harness the potential of AI while respecting its limitations. Only by balancing this delicate tightrope can AI be realised profitably and successfully in a world where we should still not give up our human intelligence.

Orchestrating technologies for seamless BPM

The use of business process management software (BPM software), process mining, process intelligence, robotic process automation, and any other process optimisation technologies not described in detail here are ideal for or-

BPM software as well as process mining, process intelligence and robotic process automation are ideally suited as integral tools.

chestrating them in an integrated business process management approach (also often referred to as a BPM platform approach). They should not only be but must also be systematically integrated into the entire process life cycle and, thus, into a business process improvement process (BPIP).

An integrative approach enables seamless integration and interoperability between these systems, ensuring data consistency and eliminating redundancies. In addition, this integration allows for a comprehensive insight into the entire business process landscape along the entire process life cycle, from process definition and architecture to documentation, analysis, requirements management, and optimisation (including automation) through to retrospective and prescriptive real-time optimisation and monitoring.

In addition, an integrative approach to these technologies facilitates collaboration and knowledge sharing between the various stakeholders. It provides a central repository for process mapping, process analysis and automation and promotes a culture of continuous improvement and innovation with a common language.

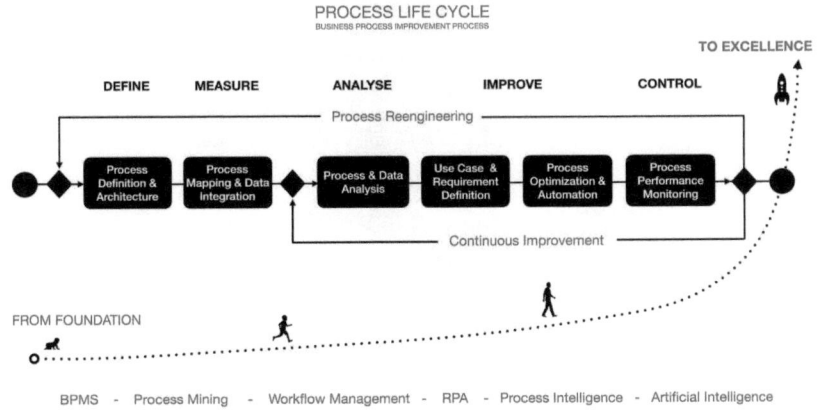

11. Process life cycle: Seamless integration of technologies and methods

Furthermore, such an approach offers more efficient scalability, allowing organisations to adapt quickly and flexibly to changing business requirements and technologies. It also contributes to a coherent and holistic overview of an organisation's business process world, which (finally) meets the requirements for managing process and complexity (see Figure 11).

After all, if a central instance manages and orchestrates such BPM tools and technologies, enormous risks can be reduced, and licence, implementation, and maintenance costs can be saved.

In summary, business process management software (BPM software) is a conductor that orchestrates processes and technologies for process optimisation into a harmonious symphony. An integrated business process management system also eliminates silos and creates an ecosystem of continuous, holistic and sustainable process development. With technolo-

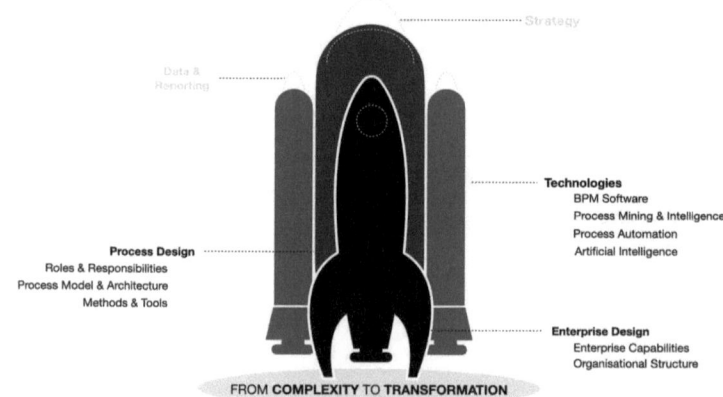

12. Process Excellence Enterprise: From technology to valuable platforms

gies such as process mining and intelligence, business intelligence, robotic process automation, artificial intelligence and other technologies not explicitly explained here, BPM offers a powerful arsenal of tools for intelligent process optimisation and transformation.

Process intelligence with real-time monitoring and predictive analytics ensures continuous improvement. Combining BPM methods (e.g. Six Sigma) with these BPM technologies unleashes the full potential for process excellence. The challenge of process automation with robotic process automation is to understand the needs and capabilities of the business and to strike a balance between process optimisation and automation for legacy processes. AI technologies further improve BPM by accelerating process modelling, providing insights and automating complex tasks. The systematic integration of these technologies into an integrative business process management approach creates a comprehensive, scalable and collaborative BPM framework that promotes innovation and adaptability. This holistic approach reduces risk, saves costs and ideally positions organisations for agile and data-driven process management. These tools are extremely promising, but they must also be implemented carefully and holistically to realise the true treasures of a complex process world while keeping risks under control. Therefore, managing these tools within a BPM approach is critical to success and is an increasingly crucial key enterprise capability.

Get ready ✈ *for another adventure in space aboard the remodelled spaceship Enterprise! During the integration of the business process management software, our crew had a few funny problems. Poor Freddy couldn't keep up with the turbo speed, but don't be afraid because we discovered ingenious* additions to process mining & intelligence, robotic process automation, and artificial intelligence. Say goodbye to the old 1.9 turbo hamster wheel and say hello to Freddy's 4.0 turbo cougar drive! Watch the spaceship Enterprise hurtle through the cosmos faster than you can say, 'Houston, we've got some turbo drives'. As our crew embarks on exciting new adventures, they say goodbye to mind-numbing tasks thanks to targeted RPA solutions. Freed from the shackles of monotonous, rule-based work, they can now concentrate on solving cosmic mysteries in the great unknown. But wait, that's not all. Jimmy, the technical genius, has modernised the system monitoring technology. We get real-time data on engine performance, allowing us to traverse the galaxy like never before. We've also hired a new co-pilot named Chatty P., who is independent and ready to take on any challenge. As the most innovative spaceship in the universe hops from star to star, the crew is happy and cheerful. Well, almost everyone. Poor Jimmy's control displays start to show massive cost increases, which depresses him. Have we lost ourselves in the glare of the entire Milky Way? Have we lost sight of the big picture, become too wrapped up in the beauty of new technologies, and are we possibly missing the overarching goals of our MISSION POSSIBLE? Now it's Nelly's turn, and it's time to boot up our state-of-the-art navigation system. The only thing missing are the coordinates.

'Technology is just a tool. When it comes to getting children to work together and motivating them, the teacher is the most important thing.'

- Bill Gates -

5. From **strategy** to **reporting**

A dynamic and well-defined strategy is the Holy Grail for any organisation that wants to conquer the business world. It is a compass that provides a clear direction and fills every decision with purpose and ambition. A strong strategy creates a unified vision that unites employees and departments and promotes collaboration and coordination within an organisation. It also gives organisations a competitive advantage, enabling them to take a unique market position and delight customers with their unique offerings. Strategy is the driving force behind effective resource allocation, ensuring that investment and effort are focused on the areas where it will have the most significant impact. In an ever-changing landscape, a solid strategy enables organisations to surf the waves of uncertainty, adapt quickly to new opportunities and ride the wave of success. It is the roadmap to success and guides organisations towards their long-term goals with unwavering determination. So, harness the power of a clearly defined strategy and open the doors to new opportunities!

In many organisations, BPM-oriented areas and initiatives are still very much focused on harmonising and standardising business processes, primarily to achieve cost savings and shorten lead times. This is fine and understandable, but what is regularly underestimated is the anchoring with the enterprise strategy, which, derived from this, consists of objectives that still need to be fulfilled beyond the standardisation and harmonisation of processes. For example, business processes have different characteristics, and the question arises as to which digitalisation projects can be used to generate new customer-added values via processes or which processes ensure compliance with requirements and laws essential for fulfilling the business model. Simply focusing on the potential for standardisation and harmonisation does not do sufficient justice to a process excellence approach. In addition to anchoring a BPM approach with the enterprise strategy, it is necessary to categorise processes to differentiate between processes with a high influence and a lower influence on the enterprise strategy. Differences in the frequency of execution, cost and resource commitment, (digital) value creation potential and regulatory and risk-based correlations must also be taken into account.

The strategy chessboard: from vision to victory

Developing and defining a strategy involves several essential steps. Firstly, it is crucial to comprehensively analyse the organisation's internal and external environment through a SWOT analysis. In addition to aspects such as brand, customers, market, competitors, products, services, risks and financial resources, the SWOT analysis should also include the current status of the aspects mentioned in the previous chapters, such as the enterprise capabilities, organisational structure, processes, roles and technologies. This enables a clear understanding of the organisation's position in the market and in general.

Now it is time to get down to business and define and describe the desired and future state within the framework of a vision, a mission and the core values that guide the organisation. The strategic objectives are derived from the vision and mission and are therefore aligned with the organisation's purpose and agreed with executive management. Once the vision, mission, core values and goals are defined, the GAP analysis is performed to identify the discrepancies between the current state of the organisation and the desired future state. This analysis helps to determine what needs to be done to close gaps and achieve the desired results. The next logical step is to define an action plan that sets out the necessary measures, responsibilities and deadlines for achieving the objectives. At this point, it is advisable to evaluate the impact of the project portfolio on the relevant business processes and establish a link between the process world and the enterprise strategy. Unfortunately, running such projects separately from process management has become common practice, which regularly leads to redundancies in the process world and weakens process management within the organisation. Therefore, projects and initiatives with a robust process-related influence should be categorised accordingly and at least supported, if not driven, by BPM-oriented departments. The results of this evaluation are then incorporated into a strategy roadmap, which, in addition to prioritising and allocating resources, also considers the penetration of the process world.

In line with Peter Drucker's quote, 'You can't manage what you can't measure', it is essential to quantify and track the strategy's performance. Metrics make it easier to assess progress, identify areas for improvement, and effectively manage and implement change. Here, the synergies between process management and enterprise strategy are underutilised in practice despite measuring processes as a core competence (capability) of process management!

It is not a mistake to make mistakes. It is only a mistake not to recognise them in time and not to learn from them.

However, creating meaningful metrics is still challenging in a world where millions of data are generated daily. Metrics should be easily accessible, transparent, specific, measurable, achievable, relevant, and time-bound (SMART). In today's complex world, making mistakes is not a mistake. It is only a mistake not to recognise these mistakes in good time and not to learn from them.

In addition, effective and continuous communication and promoting an open, creative, self-critical and productive culture is essential for a successful strategy implementation, as this ensures that employees understand the strategy and their role in its realisation.

Of course, various challenges can arise when developing and implementing an enterprise strategy. One of the biggest challenges is adapting the strategy to the ever-changing business environment. Markets, technologies and consumer expectations constantly evolve, making developing a relevant and adaptable strategy difficult. Another challenge is the balance between short-term and long-term goals. While it is essential to focus on immediate results, a successful strategy also includes measures for sustainable business success. Specifically, in the process world of organisations, short-term success can be our future legacy for complex and complicated processes. A healthy balance between short-term process optimisation and sustainable process transformation is absolutely necessary. Finding this balance between short-term successes (e.g., revenue generation) and long-term strategic goals (e.g., transformation of processes and structures) is a complex balancing act.

Another challenge is the allocation of resources. Limited financial and human resources can restrict the ability to simultaneously implement all aspects of a strategy. This can be particularly challenging when new opportunities arise and grow faster than expected. Prioritising and deciding on the allocation of strategic resources and actions, such as the project portfolio, is a complex and conflictual process involving assessing potential trade-offs and selecting the initiatives with the most significant impact. This is especially true as this evaluation can vary significantly within an (functional) organisation. The greater the gap between the as-is and target state from the GAP analysis, the greater the conflict will be, as the balance between fundamental and sustainable changes and the fulfilment of new and short-term customer expectations is too far apart and must be mastered.

However, the biggest and most difficult challenge lies in the area of people. By nature, people tend to think and work in familiar structures. Ingrained human behaviours are like established motorways with exits and junctions that still need to be explored. As long as these exits are not sufficiently well signposted and these new destinations are not interesting and attractive enough, the established motorways will normally continue to be used and, in the worst case, expanded. Resistance to change is normal and arises from fear of the unknown, concerns about job security or simply the comfort of wanting to maintain the status quo. Beliefs serve as signposts and make it difficult to deviate from them. Creating and expanding new road connections is exhausting and difficult for humans because the brain naturally strives for efficiency and familiarity, which makes it resistant to change. New signposts, pioneers and target pictures must embrace and adapt to new approaches. Many change initiatives in organisations fail because they overlook the human aspect of change. Organisations may focus too much on the technical or structural aspects of change and neglect the emotional and psychological impact on employees. Successful change requires a comprehensive approach that considers

Resistance to change is normal and arises from fear of the unknown.

the technical, structural and human aspects of change. The tricky thing about this human behaviour is that this form of resistance is usually hidden beneath the surface, and this is also the reason why, in addition to a bottom-up approach in which employees are actively and intensively involved in the change process, a robust top-down approach with clear guidelines is inevitable and necessary for success.

In summary, the management and implementation of a strategy involves many complex aspects and must be continuously controlled and adapted. Anchoring process management with the enterprise strategy can be a win-win situation for both approaches, as both sides can utilise synergies. Overall, it makes sense in larger organisations to adapt the enterprise capability of strategy and change management to the  status quo and thus the maturity of the culture and organisation in terms of capacity and expertise because here, too, '**culture eats strategy for breakfast**'.

Dual forces: top-down vs. bottom-up

Top-down and bottom-up are like yin and yang and represent two opposing but interrelated forces that play an essential role in the natural world. The concept of yin and yang emphasises the idea that these opposing forces are complementary and cannot exist without each other. A top-down approach provides clear direction, guidance and structure for change initiatives and helps employees develop the courage to break new ground and soar to new heights. It forms the basis and creates the necessary framework for people to support the desired changes. Some of the aspects of the top-down approach have already been described. The enterprise strategy and objectives, as well as the associated enterprise capabilities and structures, which we cannot leave to chance and cannot be defined democratically, are clear areas of a top-down approach. Without a rigorous top-down approach and clear governance, it will be impossible for many organisations to leave their comfort zone and venture into the unknown. It is even quite likely that without a top-down approach, chaotic and contradictory conditions will arise, leading to a waste of valuable resources.

Without a rigorous top-down approach and clear governance, it will be impossible for many organisations to leave their comfort zone.

A bottom-up approach is, of course, no less important and is also crucial for successful change and/or transformation. Involving the workforce in the change process strengthens their sense of ownership and commitment. Organisations can tap into their valuable expertise by asking for their ideas, concerns and feedback. This approach encourages innovation and creativity, allowing for various perspectives and ideas. Furthermore, involving the workforce from the outset creates buy-in, boosts morale and reduces resistance to change. Organisations can adapt to a rapidly changing business environment by leveraging their unique insights and knowledge. Finally, a bottom-up approach promotes the sustainable aspects of change by creating a culture of continuous empowerment, improvement and learning.

A balance between top-down and bottom-up approaches unleashes the power of collaboration and diversity.

A balance between top-down and bottom-up approaches unleashes collaboration and diversity and creates the conditions for an extraordinary and transformative change process. Top-down is the organisation's GPS, and bottom-up is the fuel that empowers and motivates your people. This dynamic interplay of top-down guidelines and bottom-up commitment and creativity paves the way for a comprehensive and effective change process. It sparks a vibrant culture where every

Top-down is your GPS and bottom-up is the fuel that drives you.

voice is heard, every idea is valued, and every individual has the opportunity to contribute to a larger vision. With this harmonious blend of both approaches, organisations embark on a remarkable and inspiring journey to sustainable change and noteworthy success. Embrace the power of balance and experience the extraordinary results that await you with this approach!

Imagine you are back on the spaceship Enterprise. You need a captain who sets the direction, develops strategies, derives goals and defines values. On the other hand, you need a professional and enthusiastic team to motivate, empower and convince. In this cosmic adventure, there are bi-directional approaches that complement each other to create the perfect cosmic journey. These two approaches do not contradict each other but complement each other perfectly.

But are we flying fast enough, and are we flying in the right direction? Our control systems have many dashboards and millions of data and measurement units fed by many different new technologies and sources. Freddy thinks we're flying fast enough, but Nelly doesn't even think we're travelling anywhere because we're still zigzagging. So there's still something missing, isn't it? Let's fill in this missing puzzle piece to become a future-proof 'Process Excellence Enterprise.'

From corporate goals to meaningful metrics

Metrics have **impressive power when** it comes to implementing strategies. Think of them as guiding stars that light the way to success. With their ability to measure progress and evaluate performance, metrics are the most powerful tool. The power of metrics lies in their ability to transform raw data into actionable insights that provide teams with valuable support for informed decision-making. When metrics are aligned with goals, they pave the way to excellence, illuminate areas of improvement, and guide teams to a state of continuous growth. By promoting accountability at every step of the journey, metrics give teams a sense of ownership. Without metrics, teams risk losing sight of the big picture, stumbling through the fog of inefficiency and failing to recognise progress. Harnessing the power of metrics is not just an option but a definite must. Consider the brilliance of metrics as mandatory, as they are the key to turning the results of a strategy into a reality and making them visible.

Utilising the majestic power of metrics is not just an option, it's a must.

Metrics are the key to turning strategy into reality.

However, defining available, efficient, and meaningful metrics is a fine art, and harmonising them with the strategy is a challenge. One of the first hurdles to overcome is the struggle for clarity. It requires a thorough understanding of the organisation's goals and strategy. Without this clarity, the delicate balance between ambition and achievability threatens to collapse like a house of cards.

Another challenge is selecting the right metrics. It's like an exciting fishing trip where you must patiently wade through a vast sea of metrics from today's flood of data to find the ones that really get to the strategic core. The precise alignment between the metrics and the strategic objectives is of the greatest importance so that the teams do not follow a compass that points in the wrong direction. The core of the strategy may, as so often, yearn for market position, growth, and profitability, but the metrics selected should  measure not only these goals themselves but, more importantly, **the true and relevant drivers for them**.

It is imperative that the challenge of participation and commitment is not overlooked. Imagine a stage where every actor is unfamiliar with their role, leading to a cacophony of confusion and disorganisation. For a strategy to be successfully implemented, these metrics must be made accessible and cascaded to all stakeholders. Without a commitment to these metrics, they remain lifeless numbers in tables and colourful dashboards without their transformative power.

This is, of course, easy to say in theory, but in practice, it is a considerable challenge that puts even the most experienced strategists to the test. A central sticking point lies in the fragmentation of functional organisations. Departments, divisions and locations often work in silos, focusing on their own developed goals and metrics. These silos create barriers that impede the flow of information and collaboration, leading to conflicting target systems and priorities. The resulting competing agendas can make the process of aligning organisational metrics tense, inconsistent and compromising, leading to a dilution of the clarity and focus of strategic objectives. Simplifying the definition of metrics through process orientation can be a stimulating and helpful approach, even if process metrics do not cover all necessary metrics. Imagine gears where each tooth merges seamlessly into the next to achieve a common goal for all organisational units. By focusing on processes, the complexity of defining metrics is tamed. Process-related metrics reduce frictional losses and improve collaboration if defined along the strategically most crucial business processes and cascaded down to the functional level.

By focussing on processes, the complexity of defining metrics is tamed.

From strategy to action with cascading metrics

Strategic metrics have the characteristic that they are presented in aggregated form and, therefore, have a very high flight altitude. We need an approach that harmonises employees' efforts and promotes collective action. This is where the dynamic power of cascading metrics comes into play to drive organisations to peak performance. Cascading metrics have proven to be game changers as they effectively break down barriers and dissolve traditional silo thinking. With their ability to permeate every level of an organisation, these performance indicators catalyse collaboration and promote accountability.

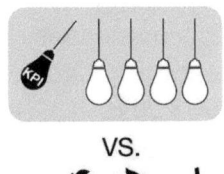

VS.

One of the strongest allies of cascading metrics is their integration into the business process world. Organisations can unleash unimagined potential by seamlessly linking these strategic indicators with day-to-day business. Business processes provide an excellent basis for cascading metrics as they have precise architectures from the highest (end-to-end) level to the lowest execution level (activity level). They thus serve as a solid basis for breaking down metrics and enable a comprehensive understanding of performance at each level. In addition, integrating metrics **The integration of metrics into business processes takes organisations to a new level of excellence.** into business processes ensures that everyone is on board and working towards the same common goals, from the management level down to the workforce. This approach fosters a culture of ownership and collaboration that drives individuals and teams to exceed their potential.

Whether you want to increase operational efficiency, promote a performance culture or take your organisation to the next level, don't underestimate the power of metrics within business processes. Let this winning combination be your secret weapon for sustainable success in the competitive business landscape. It's time to break free from the shackles of conventional and function-orientated thinking and harness the transformative potential of cascading metrics (Figure 13).

The metrics triangle, a proven paradigm encompassing cost, quality and time, is still considered the prime example for defining and deriving metrics. This triumvirate of metrics simply embodies the fundamental pillars on which organisations thrive. It epitomises the balance between cost efficiency, uncompromising quality and timely performance. Whilst contempora-

13. From strategy to a cascaded metrics system

ry data-driven approaches may be alluring, it's crucial to re-member the metrics triangle's enduring significance and strai-ghtforward application.

So, let's not be tempted by unnecessary complexity as we navigate the intricacies of the modern business and data world. In our pursuit of excellence, let us refocus on the es-sentials to ensure that our organisations are based on timel-ess principles and equipped for sustainable growth.

Of course, this assumes that the organisation already has a well-developed process management system and that pro-cess structures, responsibilities and process management technologies are in place, but this is precisely why processes are the backbone of an organisation!

Precise data management for effective and correct metrics reporting

By cascading metrics, organisations can ensure that reporting is aligned from both the top down and the bottom up, enabling a comprehensive understanding of performance at all levels. Cascading metrics mean that high-level strategic objectives are aligned with specific operational metrics. This ensures that management can track the organisation's overall performance while each level of the organisation breaks down the metrics and monitors them proportionately. This alignment also facilitates effective reporting as it establishes a clear link between specific measures at the operational level and the overarching strategic objectives at the management level.

Therefore, effectively managing data and metrics is a challenging task and another enterprise capability critical to success. One aspect emphasising this capability's importance is that influential metrics are often based on data from different source systems. We generate millions of pieces of data and information, which will continue to increase due to the growing number of digital systems. Getting lost in this deep sea of data is very easy, and the risk of being led by incorrect or inaccurate data will increase. Therefore, proper data management is crucial to ensure the accuracy, consistency and integrity of the data used to calculate metrics.

The management of metrics requires the establishment of robust frameworks.

The management of metrics requires establishing robust data policies and processes for providing, structuring, integrating and processing data from various source systems. To this end, organisations must implement data governance frameworks that ensure data ownership, quality standards and validation procedures. Through proactive data management, organisations can ensure that the metrics derived from this data are reliable and reflect the organisation's actual performance.

Effective metrics management also involves defining clear responsibilities and roles for data management. This ensures that specific individuals or teams are responsible for maintaining data integrity, resolving data discrepancies, and calculating metrics. Coordinating these roles with other process management roles is advisable to avoid redundant or overlapping responsibilities, **as data and information are ultimately generated, processed, and changed in business processes**.

Another aspect of data and metrics management is using technological tools and solutions to rationalise data collection and processing. The introduction of efficient data management systems such as data warehouses, data catalogues, or business intelligence platforms considerably simplifies the process of calculating metrics. It helps to ensure that timely and accurate information is available for reporting.

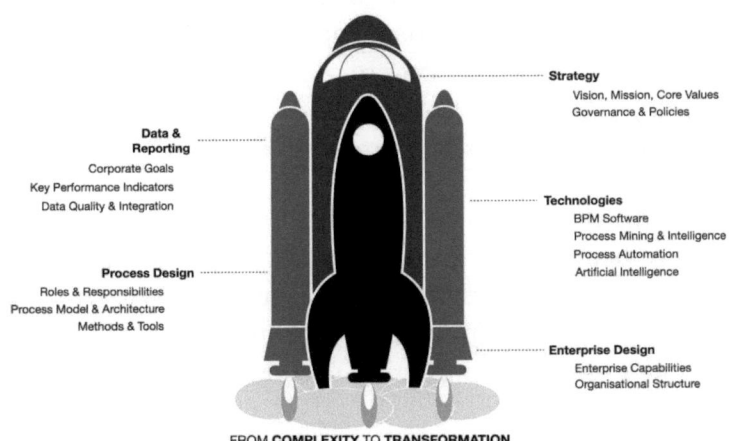

Strategy
Vision, Mission, Core Values
Governance & Policies

Data & Reporting
Corporate Goals
Key Performance Indicators
Data Quality & Integration

Technologies
BPM Software
Process Mining & Intelligence
Process Automation
Artificial Intelligence

Process Design
Roles & Responsibilities
Process Model & Architecture
Methods & Tools

Enterprise Design
Enterprise Capabilities
Organisational Structure

FROM **COMPLEXITY** TO **TRANSFORMATION**

14. Process Excellence Enterprise: From strategy to reporting

Take Away

It is often debated whether a top-down or bottom-up approach is the right one, but the two methods are not contradictory and are absolutely necessary at the same time. Top-down and bottom-up are like yin and yang, i.e., two opposing and equally interconnected poles that are closely interlinked.

To summarise, a comprehensively formulated, implemented and communicated strategy is the cornerstone for defining and cascading key figures. The connection between process and data management is essential, as processes and data are closely linked. Organisations can gain profound insights and drive transformative change by harnessing the power of data and processes in perfect harmony. However, organisations must overcome traditional structures and develop the necessary enterprise capabilities. Data and metrics, like processes, need to be structured and organised. In this way, data and metrics become co-pilots and help organisations to achieve their goals more effectively.

Despite top-down approaches and metrics, we must not neglect the people in the organisation. Further measures are needed to involve employees and allay their fears by keeping them well informed, involving them in new approaches and procedures early and preparing and empowering them for the new challenges.

Exploring ▸ *the galaxy is like looking at the stars in the night sky, where we sometimes get lost in the brilliance of individual stars. In this galaxy full of stars (opportunities), a clear direction (strategy) with precise coordinates (goals), as well as perfor-*

mance and progress indicator metrics, are the missing ingredients that will lead us to our goals and successes. This was the missing piece of the puzzle because what good is a state-of-the-art spaceship with the best navigation equipment if we don't know the coordinates of our mission? With the coordinates, Nelly can now use her navigation systems, and Jimmy can compare the costs and effort with the available resources and overall objectives. The spaceship is now ready for take-off. Freddy, Nelly, Jimmy, and everyone else have brought their skills, responsibilities, processes and technologies along the **Mission Possible** up to date, and the spaceship Enterprise is 'purring like a kitten'.

> **'When we lost sight of the goal, we worked harder than before.'**
>
> *- Carl Gustav Jung -*

6. The **TOM** as the basis for a **Centre of Process Excellence**

A customised Target Operating Model (TOM) aligned with the organisation's goals is the epitome of excellence in modern organisations. It is the art of imagining, designing and executing a future state for an organisation to optimise its operations, capabilities and performance. The TOM is inspired by aligning and connecting strategies, enterprise capabilities, responsibilities, processes, technologies, and people to unleash the full potential of innovation and growth. In short, the TOM is a strategic masterpiece that aligns organisations to their goals with unrivalled clarity, efficiency and agility. It is the blueprint for success that revolutionises businesses and paves the way for an exciting journey of transformative possibilities. A TOM, therefore, provides a clear vision of how the organisation works and how the different functions should interact and collaborate to achieve the desired results.

In turn, a Center of Process Excellence (CoPE) is a flagship in the field of organisational excellence. Driven by a relentless pursuit of operational efficiency and innovation, a CoPE serves as a beacon of expertise in the difficult art of process management. At its core, a CoPE is responsible for designing and improving an organisation's processes. It scrutinises existing processes meticulously and identifies bottlenecks as well as inefficiencies hindering productivity. The impact of a CoPE goes beyond analysing and designing. It also plays the vital role of creating process transparency and ensures accurate and up-to-date process mapping, guidelines and documentation. By carefully maintaining these 'libraries', a CoPE ensures that all stakeholders have access to the most up-to-date information, fostering a culture of transparency and consistency. With a passion for knowledge sharing, a CoPE imparts its knowledge through customised training and education concepts. Through workshops, seminars and training sessions, stakeholders are educated and equipped with the skills and abilities they need to tackle process-related tasks and challenges. In its ambitious pursuit of continuous improvement, the CoPE establishes metrics that measure success. Regular monitoring and measurement against these performance standards enables a thorough review of process performance and enables organisations to identify areas for improvement and achieve continuous efficiency and effectiveness gains. The CoPE also acts as the guardian of process management governance and compliance by ensuring that processes comply with relevant regulations, industry standards and organisational policies. By establishing robust governance frameworks, conducting audits and providing guidance, the CoPE protects and fosters an environment of trust and accountability. Recognising the transformative potential of BPM technologies, CoPE works seamlessly with IT departments to identify opportunities for process automation and technology adoption. By utilising automation tools and other BPM technologies, processes are streamlined, manual effort is reduced, and a new era of efficiency and effectiveness is ushered in.

But why should the long-established target operating models (TOM) be touched or changed when introducing a CoPE? There are several reasons for this because organisations with a CoPE change or adapt structures, strategies and goals and introduce or expand new technologies (e.g. process mining, RPA, artificial intelligence, etc.). To this end, organisations develop or expand new enterprise capabilities (e.g. process and business intelligence). At the same time, management and support processes (e.g. demand and project management, portfolio management, process management, data management, etc.) and new methods (e.g. agility, Six Sigma, OKRs, etc.) are being introduced or adapted and given a new significance. In addition, new roles (e.g. process manager, data scientist, etc.) and responsibilities (e.g. strategy officer,

The old world and the new world no longer fit together.

process owner, data owner, chief process officer, etc.) are being defined. The old world and the new world no longer fit together. But what happens if a TOM is not adapted to these new needs and requirements? Quite simply, in these cases, friction arises in the ecosystem that makes it impossible to exploit the full potential of a CoPE.

So, a well-thought-out TOM is at the heart of every successful CoPE. This invaluable blueprint guides the CoPE towards process efficiency, clear responsibilities and roles, and flawless integration of technologies and transformation processes. Without a solid TOM, your CoPE may lack the strategic alignment and integration into its organisational structure to achieve true process excellence.

Pioneering work for a new kind of operational excellence

Introducing and establishing a CoPE is a significant task with good prospects, but it also means a massive change for organisations. Establishing a CoPE requires considerable intervention in existing organisational structures, responsibilities and processes and is therefore closely interlinked with the TOM. At best, the implementation and establishment of a CoPE should be accompanied and supported by organisational development due to the organisational and cross-divisional implications.

Here are the most important aspects and steps required for the introduction of a CoPE:

🔺 **Define the horizon | Clarify the purpose and scope of the Centre of Process Excellence:** Define the fundamental purpose of a Centre of Process Excellence and, thus, the destination of your journey towards robust process redesign, improvement and standardisation. Explore the heart of this centralised function that acts as a powerful catalyst, driving organisations to unprecedented levels of efficiency. Describe executive leadership's role and key stakeholders' importance in driving the CoPE and organisational alignment. It also defines how leaders must provide the necessary support, resources, and capacity and, thus, how the functional roles interact with the process-focused roles. Finally, evaluating adjustments to the target operating model (TOM) is necessary to integrate the CoPE seamlessly into an organisation's structures and processes.

🔺 **Leading the way | The essential roles and responsibilities within a CoPE:** Take a look into the world of governance and leadership by introducing the key players in the CoPE. Define the team of process owners, process managers and experienced professionals (e.g. data scientists) who take responsibility for implementing process-driven initiatives. Define how their unwavering commitment, fuelled by executive support and sponsorship, gives the CoPE the authority, resources and visibility to lead transformative change. Also, they must understand and define their critical role (e.g., chief process officer) to motivate the development of guiding principles and strategic priorities for the CoPE. Review the impact of the new roles on the Target

Operating Model (TOM) to enable efficient integration of new roles and responsibilities and ensure effective collaboration within the organisation.

🔥 Unleashing creativity | Mastering process optimisation methods: Unlock the secret to unleashing untapped potential by investing in and implementing effective methods and tools. Harness the transformative power of Lean Six Sigma, BPM's strategic insights, and the versatility of other modern (agile) methods that promote collaboration, ownership and transparency.

🔥 The Symphony of Collaboration | United Minds for Unrivalled Progress: Create a platform for the harmonious symphony of collaboration and knowledge sharing that emerges in a CoPE by forming process-oriented steering committees and boards. Discover how this dynamic platform brings cross-functional teams together. Witness the CoPE's important role in establishing a vibrant culture of sharing best practices, lessons learnt and remarkable success stories.

🔥 Pioneering at the technological frontier | Outstanding performance through cutting-edge tools: Explore and utilise cutting-edge technologies and innovations that can be used integratively to support and significantly accelerate the pursuit of process improvement. Discover the entire arsenal of transformative tools to maximise the organisation's efficiency. Be captivated by the visualisation of process modelling software, the facilitation of workflow management systems, the clarity of process performance dashboards and the acceleration of robotic process automation (RPA).

♠ Navigating Change | The Compass for Change Management and Training: Consider the 'secrets' of change management to navigate the organisation through the ever-changing tides of transformation. Utilise sophisticated training and communication strategies that ensure a smooth transition to new skills, processes and systems. Experience how a CoPE can revolutionise the organisation's readiness for change and ignite innovation.

♠ The pursuit of perfection | Continuous improvement and the pursuit of excellence: Explore the area of strategic, operational and cascaded performance measurement and metrics as your GPS, relentlessly guiding the CoPE towards process excellence while effectively engaging all stakeholders. Introduce feedback loops and regular reviews to adjust coordinates as goals change.

In addition to all the highly technical and organisational aspects of a CoPE, which can be worked out objectively and professionally, the most fundamental part of a CoPE introduction is overcoming resistance to change and the new form of collaboration. Even with the best change strategies and methods and appropriate management support, it should not be underestimated that change, as well as introducing a CoPE, requires time and patience. Conversely, resistance, time, and patience should never be an excuse for persistently and continuously building all those mentioned above and very extensive aspects of a CoPE because, without them, it would also not work. Nor will it help organisations avoid this resistance and the effort behind it by simply setting up the 'Centre of Process Excellence', which then operates in a new splendour within old structures. The key is a tailored approach with patience and persistence that addresses specific concerns and involves stakeholders at all levels. By focusing on open communication, engagement, training and support, you can help employees understand and accept the need for a CoPE to manage change together successfully.

The CoPE Masters and architects of transformation

Realising the full potential of process excellence requires the expertise and commitment of an exceptional team. Several key roles in a CoPE are critical in driving transformative change and helping organisations achieve best-in-class efficiency. This team forms an indispensable collective, from the visionary leaders who steer the ship to the rigorous process owners, skilled professionals and supporters who lead the way. They are passionate and committed to utilising cutting-edge methods, forging collaborative partnerships and empowering people with the necessary skills to manage the transformation. The specific roles and their responsibilities may vary depending on the organisation. Here are some general roles and functions that you will need in some form:

♠ **Executive Sponsor:** A strong leader who provides strategic direction and support to the CoPE. They ensure that the CoPE is in line with the organisation's objectives.

♠ **Chief Process Officer (CPO)**: A Chief Process Officer (CPO) is a senior executive responsible for defining the overall CoPE governance. The role of a CPO is to ensure that the organisation's processes are efficient, effective and aligned with strategic objectives at all times.

🏛 **CoPE Manager/Consultant**: A CoPE Manager/Consultant drives the day-to-day business and the establishment of the CoPE. They oversee process improvement initiatives, coordinate resources and ensure the successful implementation of process excellence and the associated governance.

🏛 **Process Owner**: Individuals responsible for specific business processes within the organisation. They identify opportunities for improvement, define operational process metrics and drive process improvements in the business processes assigned to them.

🏛 **Process Intelligence Analyst:** Professionals who analyse existing processes, identify bottlenecks and recommend process improvements. They use various techniques such as BPM software, process mining and building data models, and conduct data analyses and benchmarking to identify optimisation potential.

🏛 **Change management specialists**: Experts specialising in managing the human factor during transformative changes. They ensure smooth transitions, promote employee engagement and facilitate the introduction of new processes and tools.

🏛 **Project Managers & Lean Six Sigma Experts**: Professionals with project and process management knowledge as well as Lean Six Sigma methods. They lead process improvement projects, request and perform data analyses and apply Lean and Six Sigma principles to eliminate waste, reduce errors and improve efficiency.

◆ **Training and Development Specialists**: People who are responsible for the design and implementation of process-related training programmes. They ensure that employees have the necessary skills and abilities to manage and optimise processes effectively.

◆ **IT Architects and Developers:** Technical professionals who provide support in implementing process automation, managing process-related software/tools and ensuring the availability of the IT infrastructure required for process improvements.

This is only a limited list as, depending on the enterprise and TOM, other stakeholders such as compliance, risk management, quality management, information security, strategy management, project management, and others must also be considered.

The engine of innovation: the tasks of a CoPE

The CoPE is responsible for maintaining accurate and up-to-date process documentation, process maps and guidelines. This includes analysing existing processes, identifying rework, error rates and bottlenecks, and developing proposals to improve efficiency and effectiveness. A CoPE identifies opportunities to automate processes and introduce new BPM technologies. It works closely with IT departments to implement tools and technologies to automate processes, make workflows more efficient and reduce manual effort. A CoPE is also responsible for establishing process performance indicators, which are used to evaluate the performance of the enterprise and its processes. In addition, a CoPE develops process-related dashboards and reports to the executive board on process development. They also disseminate these metrics to business stakeholders in a precise manner.

Furthermore, a CoPE offers workshops, seminars and training on process-related topics to those involved. Finally, a CoPE ensures that processes comply with relevant regulations, industry standards and the organisation's policies by establishing a governance framework, conducting audits and providing compliance guidance to stakeholders.

Breaking chains, breaking records: positioning a CoPE

Essentially, a Centre of Process Excellence (CoPE) is a community of process consultants, managers and experts. The core of a CoPE is an autonomous and independent organisational unit that ensures and orchestrates the seamless integration of process management across different functions and departments. It is a central hub that promotes cross-functional collaboration and drives process-orientated initiatives throughout the organisation. In terms of resources, this core team represents a specialised full-time team within the business, working with extended process-related roles that are typically based in the specialist departments but belong to the CoPE community as part of a functional reporting line (dotted). Although it is also possible for these process-related roles (including process owners) to report directly to the chief process officer (CPO) or head of the CoPE and core team, this is not common practice. The reporting structure can vary depending on the size, structure, and maturity of the organisation, as well

It is crucial that the cooperation between the stakeholders involved is considered, defined and coordinated by adapting the TOM.

131

as the specific responsibilities and objectives and the scope of the CoPE. It is crucial that the cooperation between the stakeholders involved is considered, defined and coordinated by adapting the TOM, whereby horizontal, vertical and diagonal reporting lines are generally possible. Ultimately, it is advisable to strike a balance between centralisation and departmental autonomy to ensure effective collaboration and accountability.

The CoPE is headed by a chief process officer (CPO), who is responsible for its operation and conceptual and strategic direction with his core team. This role has extensive experience in process management and promotes process-related initiatives throughout the organisation. The CoPE core team, which the CPO leads, consists of process management specialists, architects, consultants, and analysts with extensive technical and methodological expertise and many years of experience in business process management (BPM).

Finally, a cross-functional and matrix-oriented implementation of a CoPE and the core team close to the executive management is crucial to drive change in line with the strategy and against resistance and to be able to move function-oriented silos towards process-oriented teams.

Take Away

Introducing a Centre of Process Excellence (CoPE) represents a radical change for organisations and their organisational structure, as a CoPE must be able to interact efficiently with all areas of an organisation. The adaptation of the Target Operating Model (TOM) is therefore unavoidable. This may cause resistance among employees who are used to the previous way of working, but everything else is just tinkering with the status quo. This is one of the reasons why organisations are often labelled as madhouses: they significantly underestimate the impact of such fundamental adjustments in the overall context of an organisation and thus generate more friction than improvement. The strategic and organisational embedding of a CoPE in the existing organisational structure, including the integration and adaptation of the target operating model, is usually a novelty and essential if absolute process excellence is to be achieved.

In summary, there is no one-size-fits-all recipe for implementing a CoPE, as organisations are designed and developed very differently in terms of culture, history, business model, size, organisational structure, etc. The desire for a perfect recipe for implementing or establishing a CoPE is understandable, but the devil is in the details. Just as we cannot simply copy grandma's recipes, we cannot copy a CoPE concept (recipe) one-to-one from organisation to organisation. However, we know the most essential ingredients that must be 'processed' with every CoPE introduction or establishment. These ingredients include integrating the enterprise strategy, further developing enterprise capabilities, rethinking organisational structures, and the associated revision of the target operating model (TOM). In addition, technologies for managing processes and complexity must be evaluated and integrated into the process life cycle of business processes.

Ultimately, it is essential to be aware that organisations that could redesign their organisational structures with a greenfield approach would look completely different today. Any intervention in an existing organisation without a fundamental redesign will remain a compromise. This means we need a good mix of patience, conceptual flair and energy to drive and realise this transformative journey step by step. Aristotle once said, 'We are what we repeatedly do, and excellence is not an act but a habit.'

> *'The greatest danger in times of turbulence is not the turbulence itself, but acting with yesterday's logic.'*
>
> *- Peter Drucker -*

C. Summary

The question of how to achieve **true** process excellence concerns many organisations. The concept behind it is not really new, but many organisations still fail to achieve it. The reason for this is too simple to be true because the introduction of business process management entails fundamental changes in the organisational DNA of many (functional) organisations. Those who believe that business process management is done by introducing a new department or new tools will have to learn expensive and painful lessons. Building process structures and capabilities involves friction and resistance as responsibilities and roles must be reorganised.

Furthermore, organisations need to learn new capabilities that they must either acquire and/or equip with sufficient capacity. Excellent processes result from collaborative teamwork that needs to be encouraged and organised. In addition, encrusted processes must be fundamentally connected with those involved in IT, quality management, strategy and project management and much more. The connection with the strategy and corporate goals through cascaded metrics is a supreme discipline that - if implemented correctly - significantly impacts an efficient and effective transformation. Of course, considering all these aspects is a huge challenge, so a clear top-down approach with executive management support is an absolute MUST.

D. Epilogue

Today's organisations are highly professional, and complex ecosystems and environmental conditions are changing faster than ever. We have to overcome the climate crisis, and at the same time, geopolitical and economic certainties are crumbling. Added to this is the dynamic development of digitalisation. In recent years, we have also had to deal with the unpredictability of a virus. All of these developments (and many more) do not exist in isolation but in a complex interplay. The capacity of organisations to adapt to a rapidly evolving environment is becoming an increasingly pivotal determinant of organisational success. However, the development towards a more flexible organisation requires a great deal of determination, overview and perseverance, as changes of this magnitude always represent changes to existing systems.

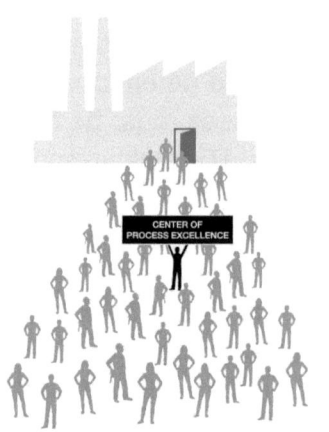

The pace of adaptation of many organisations must keep pace with rapid technological, geopolitical, economic and legal developments. However, the current structures of most organisations are not prepared for this. The requirement to continuously optimise processes and structures, as well as constantly adapt to new goals and circumstances, is at odds with traditional approaches and creates uncertainty and resistance. More than ever, processes are becoming the backbone of organisations and form the DNA of competitiveness. Indeed, we need much more than just introducing new technologies and the hope that they will solve our challenges, although they will undoubtedly make a significant contribution. Organisational change is multidimensional and takes place vertically, horizontally and diagonally at many levels of an organisation. Those who truly and seriously intend to make their organisation more efficient and effective and who want to drive real change to new shores need to do more than create a **new isolated** concept or department and give them a fancy new title like 'Center of Process Excellence'. It requires profound and fundamental changes to the organisational DNA and the target operating model (TOM). It requires a link to strategy, objectives and metrics. It requires top-down support and massive change management measures. It also requires new competencies, skills, processes, responsibilities and technologies that must be coordinated smoothly. It also requires the strategic and organisational involvement of stakeholders with whom close cooperation must be endeavoured. And, of course, it requires teamwork and team spirit!

Therefore, Process Excellence is **NOT** an 'isolated' concept or a new method that only affects selected employees in an organisation but a new management approach that involves the organisation as a whole.

It is undoubtedly possible to write separate books from each chapter and sometimes even from individual paragraphs. This alone shows how fundamental and extensive this change, or rather **TRANSFORMATION,** is. Conversely, this is **not** atomic physics and considering the core elements (see Figure 15), process excellence is a MISSON POSSIBLE. So be bold, stay motivated and ensure you are in good shape. Think big and act in continuous steps, and remember that 1,000 miles always start with the first step. So, what are we waiting for?

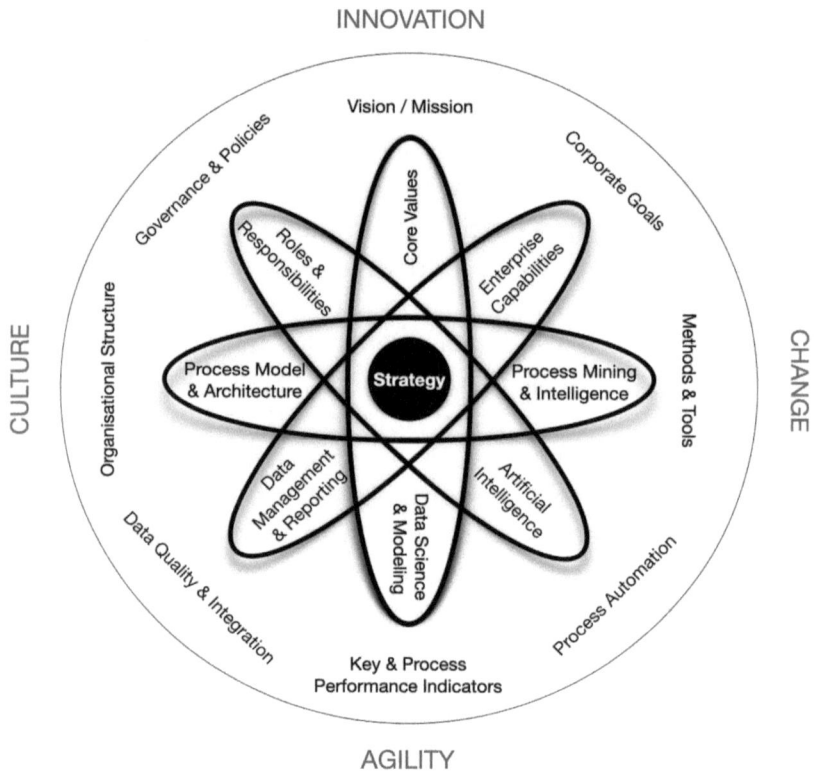

15. Core elements of process excellence

'The future depends on what you do today.'

- Mahatma Gandhi -

E. List of abbreviations

Abbrevia-tion	Language: EN
ACM	Agile Capability Model
AI	Artificial Intelligence
BI	Business Intelligence
BPIP	Business Process Improvement Process
BPM	Business Process Management
BPMS	Business Process Management System
CAPA	Corrective and Preventive Action
CBSD	Capability Building for Security and Development
CMM	Skills maturity model
CMMI	Capability Maturity Model Integration
CoPE	Centre of Process Excellence
CPO	Chief Process Officer
DCMM	Digital Capabilities Maturity Model
EAM	Enterprise Architecture Management
IMS	Integrated Management System
IoT	Internet of Things
ML	Machine Learning

PI	Process Intelligence
PPI	Process Performance Indicator
QMS	Quality Management System
RPA	Robotic Process Automation
TOM	Target Operating Model

About the authors

Etienne Kneschke

 Etienne Kneschke is the Executive Director of Business Process Management with extensive experience in business process management and continuous process transformation. His passion is developing business process management (BPM) further as a holistic management approach. His focus lies in the organisational anchoring of BPM and the application and combination of process intelligence and business process management methods and tools to increase efficiency and competitiveness. Furthermore, he focuses on integrating other management systems into an integrated management system.

- LinkedIn: www.linkedin.com/in/etienne-kneschke-a56894b2

Simon Geisenberger

 Simon Geisenberger is an experienced consultant with a background in business process management and the application of Lean Six Sigma across multiple industries. He has successfully navigated various challenges in implementing BPM technologies and is currently focused on driving process intelligence initiatives and integrating management systems for sustainable and holistic business management.

- LinkedIn: www.linkedin.com/in/simon-geisenberger-a966078